ADDICTION

A New Approach To Recovery

by John E. Smethers, Ph.D.

Addiction: A New Approach to Recovery

1st Edition 2017
ISBN-13: 978-1-906628-75-8
Published by CheckPoint Press, Ireland

CHECKPOINT PRESS, REPUBLIC OF IRELAND
EMAIL: EDITOR@CHECKPOINTPRESS.COM

WEBSITE: WWW.CHECKPOINTPRESS.COM

CheckPoint
Press

ADDICT -ION+

John E. Smethers Ph.D.

A NEW APPROACH TO RECOVERY

This book is dedicated to my Family

Lynda, Kenny, Kayla, and Jeren Castenada

John E. Smethers, Ph.D.
904 S Second Ave., Barstow, CA
Phone: 760-256-8266
Web Site: www.JohnSmethers.com
Email: gwakwa@gmail.com

CONTENTS

FOREWORD

Are there people whose lives haven't been touched in some way by addiction? If there is, they are few and far between. Everyone knows somebody that's had problems with either drugs or, more commonly, alcohol. Whether it's alcohol, drugs, sex, gambling, or any other kind of addiction, it's still addiction and those who are addicted are addicts. The image of an addict isn't what it used to be, but most addicts still consider the term 'addict', when applied to them, an epithet. Most of them rather be referred to as recreational drug users–at least that was the case with me and many of those I used drugs with. Alcoholics especially resent being referred to as addicts because they believe the term refers to drug use only. If self-diagnosed alcoholics are asked if they're addicted to alcohol, they'll inevitably answer yes, but if you ask them if they're addicts, they'll say no because 'addict' to them means drug addict. The fact is, alcohol is a drug, and those who are addicted to alcohol are addicts. I'll be using the terms *addict* and *addiction* when referring to that population in general. When referring to addicts using the alchemical process of recovery, I'll use the term partisan, which is defined as "an adherent or supporter of a person, group, party, or cause, especially a person who shows a biased, emotional allegiance." Ubiquitous as this problem is, it's amazing how little the average person knows about it. Take for example a family whose youngest member has Tourette syndrome. The parents will go to any lengths to learn about the disorder. They'll browse the Internet, read magazine and journal articles, books, and seek advice from wherever or whoever they can. However, if a family's youngest member is afflicted with addiction, the family members won't usually do the research like the family with Tourette syndrome did. Instead, they'll chastise, denigrate, fear, criticize, and often banish them, rather than go to the trouble to learn about the dynamics of addiction and find out what they should and shouldn't be doing. Those who recover usually do so through some type of process such as counseling, rehabilitation centers, or self-help groups such as 12-step programs.

The bulk of this book focuses on a succession of stages of recovery using the ancient art of alchemy as a process. Originally, alchemy was a form of chemistry and speculative philosophy practiced in the Middle Ages and the Renaissance, and concerned principally with discovering methods for transmuting baser metals into gold and with finding a universal solvent and an elixir of life. Then and now, the process of alchemy is the transmuting of a common substance, usually of little value, into a substance of greater value.

Once partisans have been through the alchemical process of recovery, they'll be of more value than they were before they started. One of the sections of chapter one will explain how.

From grammar school through high school, teachers periodically made comments on my grade reports such as, "John is a capable student but he will not apply himself." They were right. I did just enough to get to the next grade. My dad wouldn't let me quit school like many of my friends did. Because I was 17 during my entire senior year, I needed parental consent to drop out. Though I wasn't enthusiastic academically, my father still managed to instill a value for education that would surface in my life almost 30 years later.

My lack of academic initiative was exacerbated by the ethos of the 1950s. Rock and Roll and James Dean was spurning out a breed of rebels that turned into the hippies and druggies of the 60s. So it was with me. In 1956 when I was eleven years old, upon entering junior high school, I started drinking on weekends. Unlike youngsters of later generations, I didn't start experimenting with drugs until the summer of my high school graduation in 1962. I certainly would have if it was offered to me. In a nutshell, I went to a party when I was eleven and didn't get back until I was 45. Over a period of more than 30 years, there was scarcely a time when I wasn't doing time, paying fines or restitution, doing community service, serving probation or parole, pending court, or suffering the loss of my driver license. I considered those repercussions 'dues' that I had to pay to continue to live the way I wanted to.

My parents were awesome. Being their only child, I pretty much got whatever I wanted and did whatever I wanted to do--they were not strict disciplinarians, though I did spend my share of the time on restriction. Nor was I abused in any way; therefore, I don't blame them for my drug and alcohol use. I got high to have fun. Having fun was my goal in life and I avoided responsibility like it was a germ.

By the end of my 15th summer in 1960, I was an alcoholic. Three times within a six- month period, I landed in jail. Each time I had been drinking. My first night in jail was for Curfew. Probably the most significant thing about my first arrest was meeting a new friend who remains one of my best friends today. Jim and I had one hell of a good time in that jail cell, climbing around on the bars like monkeys, tearing up the mattresses for cotton ball fights, and yelling obscenities at the cops. From that point on, going to jail wasn't much of a threat. A week later another friend and I were busted for petty theft--stealing milk off of someone's porch because our mouths were dry from drinking Ripple wine all night. Eight months later, I got my first DUI on my Cushman motor scooter. My driver license was revoked before I got it. I was Jailed again the night after graduation in 1962 for trespassing and again later that year for stealing hubcaps. There were five more charges in 1963 for minor alcohol-related offenses, two of which got me 60 days in the county jail.

Once incarcerated at Glen Helen Rehabilitation Center near San Bernardino, two of my friends joined me there. We played practical jokes on each other, met new drug connections, and planned what we were going to do when we got out. It was not an unpleasant experience. Not only was being jailed for the night not much of a threat, serving time wasn't either. After I was released, one of my friends asked, "Well, how did you like it?"

I smiled and said, "I liked it." Compared to what I was expecting, I did like it. To me, it was like being in a summer boy's camp. My friend looked at me like I was crazy. I don't think he believed that I liked it. From what I understand, Glen Helen isn't the camp snoopy it used to be.

I was a happy kid, a happy-go-lucky teenager, and later a relatively happy drug addict. So why did I quit? Because my life was going nowhere, my family was concerned about me, and I knew my mind and body wouldn't take the abuse much longer, so after more than 30 years of drug and alcohol addiction, I quit. It was a process, however, rather than simply a decision. The process I used was AA and NA. Would I change anything if I had it to do over again?

No!

Why not?

Because I wouldn't be who I am today if my life had been lived differently. I certainly wouldn't be writing this book and the two before it. In my opinion, happiness is part of a temperament that is innate. Of course, life circumstances can alter that, but I believe that the basic temperament is static. If trauma doesn't strike, and we have had a stable and loving foundation in early childhood, most of us are capable of handling most of life's encumbrances. That's my opinion, anyway. However, I don't believe I could've remained very happy if I hadn't stopped. Trauma–either physical, mental, or spiritual would have inevitably struck.

Before I elaborate anymore on my shadow side, I should comment on the shining star of my life--my daughter Lynda. We lost her mother when she was four years old, so before and after and between wives, I raised her. She and I agree that my drug and alcohol addiction during her childhood has not damaged her. She inevitably became an addict herself, however, but she found recovery after only five years of drug and alcohol abuse. She got clean and sober before I did, and then she hoped and prayed that I would also find recovery. Today, Lynda and I are best friends, and she has brought two more shining stars into my life.

Fortunately, my two grand kids will never have to see me the way my daughter did. They'll never have to watch the police take me out of the house in handcuffs like my daughter did. They'll never have to control their behavior according to what drug I was taking like my daughter did. And they'll never have to endure being embarrassed in public like my daughter did. The most important thing I can share with you today, is that it hasn't been necessary for me to take a drink or put a needle in my arm since 7 May 1990 (my last relapse date), and for that I am eternally grateful.

I have been arrested over 40 times for various misdemeanor and felony offenses, served five county jail sentences, many formal and summary probations, and a three-year state prison sentence. Fortunately, I was released from parole early for collegiate scholarship and compulsive attendance in 12-step meetings. Since then I have become responsible and accountable for my actions, which I wasn't previously capable of.

Addicts have an automatic denial system, especially when it comes to their addiction or when they've been accused of something. Most of the more than two million inmates in our country's prisons are innocent. Or so they say.

Before I went to prison, my querulous old friend Jack called me on the phone to explain-- or whine (most drug addicts are chronic whiners) about being arrested for a burglary he didn't commit. He carried on for five minutes about the injustice of it all. The whole time he was ranting on, I thought about the thousands of burglaries he had gotten away with. Finally, I asked: "Jack, why are you so outraged about this?"

"Johnny, I didn't do it! God damn them! The bastards are trying to frame me."

I calmly replied, "Well Jack, what about all those burglaries you got away with over the last 25 years?"

"What? Don't get carried away Johnny. The fact is, I didn't do it. This charge doesn't have anything to do with what I did before." He dismissed my question as ridiculous.

While I was in the county jail, I overheard the following conversation: "Ya know Frenchy, I wouldn't be here for robbing that liquor store if the damn clutch wasn't bad in that old Chevy of mine. Just as I was taking off, the motor died. I got it started, then it died again. That happened three times. By the time I made it to the corner, there were red lights everywhere."

"I hear ya, bro, if my wife hadn't turned me in, I wouldn't be here either," replied Straight Razor.

I could identify with those middle-aged bikers, because I had all too often placed the blame for my behavior outside of me. It would have been a waste of time to say, "Frenchy, you wouldn't be here for robbing' a liquor store if you hadn't been robbing' a liquor store." It's strange, but that obvious statement is absurd to them. So it was with me.

While having a beer on my night off in the bar where I was a bartender, one of our regular customers asked if I could get him a quarter gram of meth. I said no. Later he asked again. Again I said no. However, when he asked me again around one o'clock in the morning, I knew that there was some in the bar, so I got the drugs for him. He was an under cover policeman. I fought the sales charge in a jury trial and lost. I took it all the way through the court of appeals, and lost that too. I was entrapped. It was not my fault. They were picking on me. The truth is, if I hadn't been selling drugs, I wouldn't have gone to prison for selling drugs. However, like Jack and those bikers, I was incapable of being accountable for my actions.

I was 45 years old before I made it to state prison. I had been knocking on the door for twenty years or more, however. As the judge looked at my rap sheet he said, "I can't figure out why you've never been sent to prison." Then he looked at me and said, "furthermore, I can't believe that I'm sitting here trying to talk myself out of sending you to prison now."

My rap sheet didn't have violent crime on it. Though there are a couple burglary charges and a robbery charge, they were investigation charges and didn't result in conviction; in fact, they didn't get past the arraignment or preliminary hearing stage. Most of my offenses were drug and/or alcohol related. I believe that's why judges were hesitant to send me to prison. But by the time this judge viewed my rap sheet, there were 40 charges that took up several pages. As it turned out, I am glad he sent me to prison.

A few months after I arrived on the prison yard, there was an experimental program starting called Project Change. It was a nine-week education and therapy program designed for pre-release inmates. On the flyer was a request for interview. I knew that I would never terminate parole successfully unless I refrained from the use of drugs and alcohol, so I filled out the request form and interviewed for a place in the program. I only wanted to remain abstinent for as long as my parole lasted, then I planned on returning to life as I knew it before I was incarcerated, which was a fun-loving, dope-fiend, party-animal.

While I was a bartender prior to going to prison, two of my friends came in frequently and drank soda. "What's up with this, Jerry?" I asked.

"I'm on parole. If I don't give my parole officer any dirty urine tests or I don't have any brushes with the law, I'll get off parole early." Jerry and Lisa both got off parole 13 months after their releases, so I was determined to do the same.

I was accepted into Project Change six months prior to my release date. Since the program was just starting, they needed to fill the dorm that was allocated for the program. Later, only inmates in their last 60 days were eligible. A month later I got a clerical position in the program. Never having used a computer, I found an inmate in the education department who tutored me until I was familiar with the word processing program on CDC's Apple computers. Once I was proficient, I typed questionnaires, work sheets, and other classroom material. We held classes five days a week in the TV room, and part of the dorm was also converted for classroom activities.

Another reason I volunteered, was for the fringe benefits. Project Change students went to chow first, and were first in line for commissary and linen as well as mail call. I am surprised that more inmates didn't volunteer, if for no other reason than for the fringe benefits.

The letters I received from Lynda, my 21-year-old daughter, even prior to my enrollment in Project Change, were motivational and rife with AA cliches and jargon. She seemed genuinely happy being clean and sober. I was not much of a father to my daughter and even less of a son to my mother. I had caused them more anguish than I could ever hope to make up for; However, once I started digesting all the literature I was typing and reading, and started taking a sincere interest in the Project Change program, I also started feeling the guilt associated with the wreckage of my past. I found myself seriously considering a life without drugs and alcohol, rather than just a temporary abstinence until I got off parole. I started to really want it, not for me, but for my family. After Lynda started reading my letters, now rife with AA cliches and jargon, her return letters were so full of hope, encouragement, and happiness, that I became that much more determined to stay clean. She and my mom were so proud of me that I absolutely could not let them down after everything I had put them through.

A mother's love knows no bounds in many cases. When my mom died, my aunt said, "Johnny, your mother idolized you. To her, the sun rose and set on you. There was nothing or nobody more important to her than you." My mom continued enabling me after her death. The inheritance she left provided me with enough money to finance two graduate degrees and enough for me to live comfortably since then. She went to her grave providing for the little boy she idolized. Today, I idolize her for giving me such unconditional love. She never lost faith in me. She loved me as much when I was drinking and using as she did when I was a kid or after I got clean and sober.

After four months in the Project Change, I believed that I had recovered from a seemingly hopeless case of mind and body. I was certain that I would not drink or use anymore. However, the fact is, even among those who are certain they will not drink or use anymore, most of them will anyway. So it was with me. I relapsed three times.

Kathy, one of the teachers in the program, recognized that I had academic ability and suggested that I go to school when I got out. I said something like, "Yeah, yeah, sounds like a good idea," but I wasn't serious and she could see that. She approached me on the matter several times, practically nagging. Finally, I started giving it some serious thought. I knew that I was going to be living with my mom again when I was released. She was on her last legs, and I wanted to take care of her for as long as she had left. I figured going to school would keep me busy with homework when I was at home. Besides, I could be of help to my mom and at the same time be doing something for myself. When Kathy heard me talking this way, she started believing that I might be serious.

In Project Change I learned that if lasting change is going to take place, one has to monitor and discipline their thought processes; therefore, if I was going to remain abstinent when I was released, I was going to have to change my thinking. As it was, almost every waking moment was spent thinking about either the bar where I was a bartender, how much fun scavenging at the dump was, the people I drank and used with, and all the women I slept with. I came to realize that being in a recovery oriented environment and having this stinking thinking going on in my head at the same time, was like having someone pushing me away and saying "come here" at the same time. I had to ask myself, how can intrinsic recovery take place with such a conflict? Chapter two focuses on thought discipline–it's the first stage of the alchemical process of recovery.

A couple months before my release date, Kathy volunteered to help me with the tedious financial aide paperwork so I could get the federal Pell Grant when I was released. I received the financial aide paperwork and she helped me with it like she promised. I was 45 years old and was going to be a college student again. I tried twice in the early '60s, both of which were failures, so I came to accept that I wasn't college material. And maybe I wasn't . . . then.

My daughter had gotten clean and sober while I was doing time in the county jail--about a year before I went to prison. She still has the letters I wrote to her during that time, and the ones I wrote from prison. After reading over them, I am amazed at all the fatherly advice I was giving her. Some of it was actually sound, but most of it was from a refractory and hedonistic loser with an inflated male ego. One thing was consistent in those letters, however. I never failed to tell her how proud I was of her and how much I loved her. If nothing else she grew up knowing she was loved. And that, I believe, is one reason why she is the epitome of motherhood to my two grand children today.

Letters she wrote to me in prison was recovery oriented, and she mentioned several of my dope- fiend friends who were showing up in AA meetings. It was comforting to know that I was going to have friends at meetings when I got out, but since I considered myself more of a drug addict than an alcoholic (I never thought of alcohol as a drug), I planned on attending NA meetings. I eventually resolved to attend both.

Today I own the home I grew up in and I have earned a few university degrees culminating with a Ph.D. Having a doctorate, owning my home, and having my car, truck, and camper paid for, are not the things that make me happy. The closeness I share with my daughter and grand children make me happy. Thinking about the time I spent caring for my mom before she died also makes me happy. But could I have sustained the happiness I had during childhood, adolescence, and through much of my drug and alcohol use had I not stopped drinking and using?

No.

Why not?

I will answer that by quoting a paragraph written above: "In my opinion, happiness is part of a temperament that is innate. Of course, life's circumstances can alter that, but I believe that the basic temperament is static. If trauma doesn't strike, and we have had a stable and loving foundation in early childhood, most of us are capable of handling most of life's encumbrances. That's my opinion, anyway." It is highly unlikely that I could've handled the mental, physical, and emotional encumbrances resulting from continued drug and alcohol use. I learned early in recovery that becoming responsible and accountable for my actions is a cornerstone of a life well lived.

My doctoral dissertation served as a foundation for my 2008 book, *Scumbag Sewer Rats: An Archetypal Understanding of Criminalized Drug Addicts.* Hopefully this book, as well as my memoir, *Addict to Academic: Recovery From 30 Years of Drug Addiction*, and *Addiction Papers: From the Perspective of Depth Psychology*, will be an inspiration to others and their families who don't believe that there is redemption for addicts.

I included this foreword to establish credibility for writing such a book. Higher education and counseling degrees don't impress addicts. Most addicts want to read or listen to someone who's been there.

≈ INTRODUCTION ≈

Addiction, the Disease Concept, and Alchemy

WHAT IS ADDICTION?

The essential feature of substance *abuse*, according to the DSM-IV *(Diagnostic and Statistical Manual of Mental Disorders)*, is a maladaptive pattern of substance use manifested by recurrent and significant adverse consequences related to the repeated use of substances. The essential feature of substance *dependence*, is a cluster of cognitive, behavioral, and physiological symptoms indicating that the individual continues the use of the substances despite significant substance-related problems. The DSM doesn't recognize the term *addiction*. I do, however, and in my opinion the best definition of addiction is: a compulsion to repeat a behavior regardless of its consequences. This definition is preferable because it covers a range of addictions beyond the scope of substances. "Recovery rates from addiction follow a model of treatment outcomes applicable to most psychologically-based disorders: one-third recover fully; one-third cyclically stop their unhealthy behavior and return to it again; and one-third do not recover." This is a blanket statement concerning recovery from abuse and dependence that can be found on the Go Ask Alice website. Jointsters, a term I coined in my book, *Scumbag Sewer Rats,* are criminalized addicts, whose criminal behavior is a result of chemical dependence and has landed them in jails and/or prisons. Their addiction and criminality are more often a developed lifestyle than a physiological dependence. Statistics by the American Medical Association (AMA), and the DSM complicate matters here. We are talking about people who have dedicated their lives to the use of drugs and alcohol, and the recovery rates for them are very low—much lower than what is stated above about abuse and dependence recovery rates.

I'm not saying that addicts don't periodically get physically addicted to substances. What I am saying is that they are more often *not* physically addicted, depending on what drugs they are using, of course. Heroin and cocaine are the most addictive psychologically and physically; however, whereas meth is highly addictive psychologically, it is not highly addictive physically. Marijuana isn't physically addictive either (except for maybe the new chemically treated marijuana), but it is certainly psychologically addictive. Therefore, it's more accurate to categorize jointsters as *addicts*, based on their criminalized lifestyle and drug use, rather than categorizing all of them as physically addicted. Now let's explore the theory of addiction as a disease.

The Disease Concept

Alcoholism was recognized as an illness by the American Medical Association in 1956. In 1966 they classified it as a *disease* because it meets the criteria of other diseases:

It is chronic—it lasts a long time.

It is progressive—it gets worse over time and can end with death.

It is incurable—it can, however, be arrested by abstinence.

It is primary—it is not just a symptom of some other underlying disorder.

In my opinion, the contention that addiction is a disease is simply conjecture. Just because the AMA says addiction is a disease, doesn't make it so.

It is chronic—so is shoplifting, it lasts a long time.

It is progressive—so is violence, it gets worse over time and can end with death.

It is incurable—so is masturbating, however, it can be arrested by abstinence.

It is primary—so is smoking cigarettes, it's not a symptom of another underlying disorder.

We can add a plethora of examples similar to the above.

Still, the medical community and society in general have accepted the disease concept and have attributed many aberrant behaviors from alcohol consumption to overeating. The disease concept was a remedy for faltering medical institutions, making available billions of dollars to the medical establishment and contributing to the growing evolution of pop-psychology.

The disease concept has infiltrated our society so thoroughly, perpetuating misinformation that damages the very people it's supposed to help. It's a disastrous situation where the theories of a few theorists were assumed as fact by the medical community, without credible evidence. It wasn't long before the disease concept was accepted by American society. Considering the history of the disease concept, we have a better understanding of why it happened the way it did.

From physicians and their patients to drug manufacturers and the popular media, there is persistent pressure to categorize any condition as a disease. Physicians, especially specialists, want to boost their standing in the medical community with credibility and income that arrives when a new condition is being labeled as a disease. Pharmaceutical companies have an obvious interest in making life's problems medical. Also, alternative therapies such as holistic medicine and acupuncture, are minimized or dismissed as unscientific. Objectionable medicalization is dangerous because of unnecessary labeling, inadequate treatment modalities, economic inefficiency, and the resulting costs when resources are prevented from treating or preventing more serious diseases. Addiction is the result of bad decisions, not a disease, and eliminating the bad decisions that addicts have made with the disease concept, is perhaps part of the reason that treatment doesn't work.

Does Treatment Work?

Like those in 12-step programs, treatment professionals claim success in the face of contradicting evidence. AA literature boasts that "Rarely have we seen a person fail who has thoroughly followed our path." The truth is, people rarely succeed even when following the path of those in 12-step programs. Approximately 80 percent of the existing treatment centers in the United States adhere to 12-Step philosophies. Not surprising, the success rate of treatment is no different in rehabs from the success rate of 12-step programs, counseling, psychotherapy, or analysis, which is approximately 3%.

While treatment professionals boast that *treatment works*, the question is, what is it that's working? The assurance that treatment works does precious little for most people who drink or use drugs too much. Of course, treatment's alternative counterpart and co-conspirators, 12-step programs, lead with the same misleading and outright assurance that their programs work. Twelve steppers conveniently claim success without any foundation. In reality the statement is a complete contradiction to empirical evidence. Both 12-step programs and treatment of *any* kind are outright failures when held to any standard but their own. However, it's apparently a matter of semantics. It comes down to who is using the word, *works*.

With the public believing that these programs are *working*, it would be a testament to helping people with substance abuse issues get clean and sober. Said another way, those who join the groups can overcome their addiction, but, after arriving in treatment, or a 12-step program, with the hopes of overcoming their addiction, those in need are told that they can never get well because there is no cure. So, what is it that's working?

With that said, the various recovery options that are available, are all there is; therefore, it would be indiscreet to say that they are a waste of time. Until someone discovers the magic bullet, we're left with what is available. I attended 12-step meetings for about 15 years, but not in the last ten years, and I'm still clean and sober today. When I was attending meetings, I didn't read the literature, I didn't have a higher power, I didn't share in meetings, and I didn't use a sponsor. However, my journey of recovery was initially made easier by attending meetings where I was able to listen to people who were like me. What I didn't agree with, I left there, and took what I could use with me.

A common cliche heard around twelve-step programs is "We are not bad people trying to get good, we are sick people trying to get better." It is my contention that addicts (again, which includes alcoholics from here on) are neither bad or sick people. They're just people who've made bad decisions that predisposed them to personify the negative poles of the *puer aeternus*[1] (eternal boy in Latin), *Puella aeternus*[2] (eternal girl), and/or the trickster archetypes in order to accommodate a lifestyle created by those bad decisions. This personi-

---

[1] The negative pole of the *puer* is characterized by a poor adjustment to daily demands, a failure to set realistic goals and to make lasting achievements in accord with these goals, and a habit of intense and short-term relationships with women. The positive pole of the *puer* is characterized by noble idealism, creative imagination, spiritual sensitivity, and often by extraordinary talent. Ironically, sometimes these positive and negative attributes emerge simultaneously.

fication is caused in myriad ways when we are indoctrinated into the mind-set associated with substance use.

So, are all of these people really sick? If they are, maybe we should start an "anonymous" program for those who are not sick (normies anonymous), because they seem to be in the minority. Apparently, there is something to be said about Andrew Weil's contention that the desire to alter consciousness periodically is an innate, normal drive, because all those *anonymous* behaviors alter consciousness to some degree. Who wouldn't, for example, like to walk around with a perpetual orgasm, as long as we could function normally at the same time? That would be the epitome of altering consciousness. Everybody would like that, but not everybody would like to be addicted to all the addictive behaviors covered in the gamut of 12-step programs and in the offices of mental health professionals. Therefore, we are dealing not with something socially or culturally based, but rather with a part biological, part archetypal (universal) characteristic of the species.

Besides, the need for altering consciousness begins at ages far too young for it to be caused by social conditioning alone. Kids playing, alter consciousness frequently, such as three to five-year-olds spinning themselves into dizziness. When I was ten or eleven years old, my friends and I would squeeze each other around the chest after inhaling and exhaling several times. Then we would lose consciousness and flop around on the floor like a fish out of water. I believe that this deep inclination to alter consciousness reflects our natural desire to transcend our daily ego-centered identity and experience something more. When these changes of consciousness interfere with normal functioning, then we need to find direction.

Many people refuse treatment for addiction because they don't believe they are sick. I agree. They are not bad and they are not sick. They need to either personify different archetypes (universal behavioral patterns) or redirect the energies of the old ones, and they need to alter consciousness in different ways. I assert that what is needed is a path to recovery from—not the *disease* of addiction, but just from addiction. Cigarette smoking is also an addiction, but it isn't labeled a disease. Chemical substances, however, are a deterrent to wholeness and stifles individuation.

Millions of people have recovered with the help of 12-step programs. There are also millions of people who have recovered by other means such as psychotherapy and/or religion. Many have even stopped using substances on their own through what is known in medical circles as spontaneous remission. However, there are others who could and would glean the many benefits of 12-step programs if they weren't bombarded with religious concepts, and having the disease concept shoved down their throats.

I am proposing a model for recovery employing the ancient art/science of

---

[2] The negative pole of the *Puella* is carefree and perhaps careless, remaining attached to the ideals of childhood, the promise of perfection, the dream of human potential without limits. She's full of optimistic smiles but unable to bear the burdens of responsibility, the tensions of compromise, and the sobering reality of adulthood. The positive pole of the *puella* is comparable to the positive pole of the *puer*.

alchemy, a model I have developed which also include other therapeutic strategies. I also explain a method that *I thought* I invented when I was in prison. I discovered later, during my education, that it was a process practiced in cognitive psychology, which, among other things, is what worked for me.

What is Alchemy?

Many of us are drawn to the mysteries of the past to enlighten the quality of the present. Mythology, astrology, the tarot, runes, and I-Ching have drawn the interest of many in recent years, and is being enjoyed and utilized in fresh and innovative ways. Ancient wisdom imbued by myths, legends and symbols can generate transformation, and transformation is what alchemy is all about. It's also what recovery is all about. More commonly known as the art of transforming base metal into gold, few people realize what a vast philosophical foundation this early science has. Alchemy is a process that continues to grow and expand, offering deeper understanding and awareness, and has a profound potential to change lives. This fountain of ancient wisdom has nourished seekers of spiritual enlightenment for centuries.

The beginning constituent of alchemy, the prima materia (primal material), is a base substance known by many but recognized only by the esoteric. The outward form of the prima materia must be destroyed because it is pure chaos. Treatment of the prima materia in the alchemical vessel by heat leads to its death, a moment known as the 'nigredo,' or blackening. With a methodical treatment and heat, the prima materia 'whitens,' indicating that the elixir is perfected in its first degree, a moment known as the 'albedo,' or whitening. To attain the gold-promising tincture of the sun, further treatment is necessary until the elixir reddens, which is referred to as the 'rubedo.' There's also a 'citrinitas,' a yellowing in the ancient process, but it isn't used in most texts that delineates the alchemical process, especially the psychological and philosophical treatises, and more specifically in correlating it to the process of recovery from addiction.

The alchemical process also transforms consciousness, which is the endeavor of depth psychology. When non-Jungians study Carl Jung's concept of the transference, they are often struck by how heavily it draws on alchemical symbolism. I won't be focusing on alchemical symbolism in my approach, but transference is always an issue between counselors and clients, sponsors and sponsees in 12-step programs, as well as psychiatrists and their patients.

In a way, sponsorship in 12-step programs is practicing psychotherapy without a license or without the supporting education. Unlike therapists, however, sponsors aren't paid for what they do. Twelve step members have been practicing psychotherapy without a license since the 1930's under the guise of sponsorship. That's acceptable, for who can heal better than the wounded healer?

With my model of transformation through the alchemical process, recovery can be achieved using my ten stages of development. Note, I am not claiming, by any means, that *Addiction: A New Approach to Recovery* is any better than any other approach or model, and I am certainly not claiming that it will be any more successful. This is not the magic bullet. It's just an option for those who have issues with traditional psychotherapy, counseling, and 12-step programs with their emphasis on God and/or higher power, the disease concept, sharing in meetings, or the tenets of 12-step literature. With this book, addicts can recover, on their own, if they adhere to everything that's suggested.

History of Alchemy

Alchemy has a history stretching back at least 2,500 years and has been practiced in Eastern, Arabic and Western societies. Historically, alchemists were more interested in the chemical techniques, others in philosophical aspects, and some saw alchemy as a path to the true meaning of Christianity, while others saw the possibilities of producing medicines and other concoctions.

Those who take issue with all the religious terminology in 12-step programs will also notice that most alchemical treatises also refer to Christianity in various aspects, but the reasons have to do with historical time periods, because those who didn't pay homage to the ecclesiastical doctrines of the time suffered for it. For example, the Swiss Renaissance physician Philip von Hohenheim aka 'Paracelsus' born in 1493 is regarded as one of the founders of modern medicine. But he was also a renowned botanist, astrologer, general occultist, *and* an alchemist. Paracelsus's desire to help the sick was genuine, but the magical means he used, and in particular the secret content of alchemy, were diametrically opposed to the spirit of Christianity.

Like I stated previously, the following formula for recovery is for those who take issue with 12-step programs, counseling, rehabs, or for those who would simply like to try something on their own. However, I am not suggesting that 12-step meetings be eliminated if attendance isn't an obstacle. It's advantageous for those in the recovery process to be continually reminded of what got them into recovery in the first place. Besides that, most addicts are more comfortable around people with backgrounds similar to their own. They identify with other addicts. The best advice I've heard concerning meetings is "take what you can identify with and leave the rest there." Too many people stop attending meetings because they don't like what they're hearing or whom they're hearing it from. It's best to make every attempt to listen to the message rather than the messenger, and seek the similarities rather than the differences of those who share in meetings. If 12-step meetings aren't an option, there are other types of support groups available for those who want to be armed as much as possible.

The Alchemical Process of Recovery

The mercurial spirit of the prima materia is otherwise known as chaos, and those entering the recovery process certainly fit that description. It is the job of the alchemist to kill the prima materia and in the process the prima materia turns into the blackening state of nigredo. This analogy sets the stage for a transformation—the first coniunctio (conjunction or union). In Alchemy, coniunctio refers to the union of our divine spirit with the soul, and finally with the body. It's been said that in the human condition the spirit, soul and body are in a way separated from each other, although they're working *with* each other. But when the Great Work has been completed, the divine spirit has been brought 'down' to shine through the soul and body and has unified itself with them, so they all form one and the same body.

The Great Works in the alchemical process of recovery are the *coniunctios*. For purposes outlined here, coniunctio is defined as reaching a birth-point in life and at the same time a death–a conjunction.

The first coniunctio begins when the ego (consciousness) discovers the reality of the unconscious psyche and makes an effort to pay attention to it. If recovery is being sought for intrinsic purposes, then the ego has acknowledged an unconscious need; therefore, the first coniunctio is the transformation from the dregs of active addiction to the *clamor* of abstinence (I emphasize clamor because early abstinence is often as chaotic as active addiction). This part of the transformation is tentative and unstable, and the most susceptible for relapse.

The second coniunctio is the transformation from abstinence to recovering. What was previously only an ideal becomes a living reality. This stage of recovering can be thought of as the whitening of the albedo—the ego having reached a new level of being. Addicts, at this new level of consciousness, should have hope.

The third coniunctio is the transformation from recovering to recovered. This can take many years, and sometimes it never happens. Metaphorically speaking, this is when the contents of the alchemical vessel have turned to gold. This is when individuation (achieving wholeness) of the alchemical process has been achieved, also referred to as the philosopher's stone. Of course, there are those who stay in the abstinence stage (albedo) indefinitely, and a regression can happen during any stage of the transformation. There are also those who return to the chaos of the prima materia that existed prior to their entry into the recovery process, which is translated as a relapse back into chaos.

The Ten Stages of Development
The first coniunctio has gotten the partisan to abstinence and to counseling or some kind of support group and/or recovery process. If recovery is being sought for intrinsic purposes, then the ego has acknowledged an unconscious need. Before the transformation to the second coniunctio can occur, addicts need to start the process of recovery. There is no specific schedule or time limit for this process, and the stages don't always have to develop in sequence.

As I've stated previously, those seeking recovery using the alchemical method, are primarily the ones who have issues with the traditional Christian sky-God—the agnostics and atheists. The word 'God' doesn't appear in the 10 stages of development. Anyone who tries this approach is encouraged to make any adaptive changes that could enhance the process, for this is a theoretical model with room for improvement. It is a work in progress.

Archetypes & Culture:

The wounded healer is an archetypal dynamic that may be constellated in a helping relationship. The term, wounded healer, derives from the mythological Asclepius, a Greek doctor who in recognition of his own wounds established a sanctuary at Epidaurus where others could be healed of their wounds. The wounded healers in the alchemical process of recovery are the addicts themselves, and addicts personify predominately two archetypes—the *puer aeternus* and the trickster. By using the alchemical process of recovery, along with whatever additional tools that become available, addicts will have likely had, or will have some kind of spiritual awakening or experience that Carl Jung said was so vitally necessary for recovery. For an exposition on spiritual experience, see chapter 11.

If addicts try to learn about a subject that they're not interest in, it won't mean anything to them. If addicts are fascinated with a subject, however, they'll acquire an emotional attachment coupled with a profound interest. As an introduction to alchemy, I suggest a little book titled *The Elements of Alchemy* by Cherry Gilchrist. In it addicts can get the basics. For a more in-depth coverage of alchemy from a Jungian perspective, I recommend two books: Jeffrey Raff's *Jung and the Alchemical Imagination* and *Alchemy* by Marie-Louise von Franz. These two books aren't easy to read unless the reader is steeped in Jungian psychology, so I suggest the book by Gilchrist first, or investing some time on the Internet getting familiar with the basics. Again, the transformation associated with recovery will be much easier if there's a profound interest in alchemy.

It is true that these things are scarcely to be understood unless one has at least a general knowledge of the terms used in the art of alchemy. Opinion is, in a way, an anticipation of the truth, fixed in the mind and often doubtful. Experiment, on the other hand, is manifest demonstration of the truth, and resolution is the putting away of doubt. We can't be resolved of doubt except by experiment, and there is often no better way to make it than on ourselves– hence, the term *self help*.

THE TEN STAGES OF DEVELOPMENT

≈ I ≈

STAGE ONE

THOUGHT DISCIPLINE

All the great leaders throughout history have taught the principle that our lives are the result of our thoughts. Buddha said, "A man's life is the direct result of his thoughts." Solomon said, "As a man thinks in his heart so is he." Happiness comes from happy thoughts, sadness from sad thoughts, success from successful thoughts, failure from failing thoughts, etc. So, our lives are controlled by our thinking. This is especially so with addicts.

Our minds have two parts, a conscious part, and an unconscious part. The conscious part is what we think and reason with. It's the part we use to plan, analyze, and make decisions. The unconscious is the part that controls all of our bodily functions, from breathing, digestion, to blood circulation. It never sleeps, and is working all the time. It's like a computer, it takes in data and processes it. It has a memory of everything that has ever happened to us, from the day we were born, to the present moment. It's nonjudgmental, doesn't know what's good or bad, and it doesn't care whether thoughts come from within or without. If addicts don't take the effort to program it positively, their unconscious will take direction from others, or any input from the environment.

When people wonder why they haven't always gotten what they wanted, or why they couldn't do certain things, then they've probably sent negative messages to their unconscious, or picked up negativity from the environment. If they aren't happy with where they are, they've usually set it up themselves. For example: if they're experiencing lack, they've probably been thinking mostly in terms of shortage. If they want to change, they must start thinking in terms of abundance. If their lives aren't going the way they want, they have the power to change. They change their lives by changing their thoughts, which are programmed to their unconscious. They start thinking of the things they want, and not of the things they don't have. They must make positive statements continually. As their thoughts improve, so will their lives. Consider this:

If you think you can, you will.
If you think you can't, you're right.

We're often told that change is uncomfortable and difficult, that it inevitably involves pain or discomfort, and that to change our lives is to struggle and fight against the status quo. There are other ways.

It seems to be a rule of nature that like attracts like. People from similar social or cultural backgrounds are drawn together by shared world-views. The rich and famous socialize within their own circle. Those with similar religious orientations congregate. And it's the same with addicts. They spend as little time as possible with normies. Birds of a feather flock together, as the old saying goes. Similarly, our thoughts tend to attract the conditions we experience. In his classic book, *The Power of Your Subconscious Mind*, Joseph Murray writes, "Everything that has happened to you happened because of thoughts impressed on your subconscious mind through belief. The habitual thinking of your subconscious mind establishes deep grooves. If your thoughts are harmonious, peaceful and constructive, your subconscious mind will respond by creating harmony, peace and constructive conditions."

The life experiences of addicts is a reflection of their inner world. The landscape they paint with their minds becomes the one they walk through daily. They are the builders, the creators of their world. They are usually unaware of this, thinking that life just happens to them, that events occur by chance, and that they are forever at the mercy of random circumstances. If they want to change their lives, they need to take responsibility for creating their own experiences. Their thoughts draw experiences of a similar quality into their lives, so it's vital that their thinking be constructive, positive, and life-changing

Sometimes there's a revolt. Because of a sudden change in a person's mental landscape, such as a paradigm shift, their lives can change enormously all at once. Years before I stopped drinking and using, I quit smoking pot. I just gave it up, and for the duration of my addiction to other drugs and alcohol, I didn't accept as much as a toke of pot whenever it was offered to me.

These sudden shifts, however, are not the ordinary course of things. Change usually takes time, it grows and matures. The tracks etched into the minds of addicts, by years, or even decades of habitual thought are not wiped away instantly. They become fainter for lack of use, like new tracks they become established, slowly but surely. Addicts need to build them step by step, and soon they become well-worn highways.

A new path can only be established by persistently being walked on. The new tracks that addicts make in their thought patterns will take time to become established, and at first those thought patterns will be weak. The normal thinking of addicts may keep drifting back to the old, negative patterns. That doesn't matter, they need to keep going and, in time, they can look back in amazement at how far they've come.

When people in general set out on new pathways, the unfamiliar routes their minds need to take can seem strange and uncomfortable. Most of them can remember a time when they found themselves in unfamiliar situations, such as getting a new job or moving to a different town or state. At first, nearly everything is uncomfortable. After a while, however, they start getting comfortable with their new situations and they start feeling better.

The reason for the uncomfortable feelings is a result of thinking, like worrying about what could go wrong, about not doing well, etc. Addicts can reduce the fear of the unknown by steering their thoughts in a more productive direction.

The following process comes from my personal experience. I'll start by discussing my dope-fiend mentality at the time I was sentenced to state prison. It was my intention to do my time, get out and serve a 13-month parole, then return to what I knew best, and what I was most comfortable with--doing drugs and alcohol as a way of life. Upon release from prison, the average length of parole is from three to four years, depending on performance. However, there are exceptions. Sometimes parolees can be released in 13 months, provided they not have any brushes with the law and not give their parole officers any dirty urine tests. Jerry and Lisa, who I mentioned in the foreword, achieved early discharges. They were inspirations to me.

A few months after I reached the prison yard at Jamestown, CA. where I was to remain for the rest of my sentence, it occurred to me that I could probably use lessons on how to stay clean, even if it was only going to be for 13 months. I started attending NA. After attending meetings for a while, I was accepted into the Project Change program that I also mentioned in the foreword.

About a month later, because of my typing skills, I landed a job with Project Change as a clerk. I typed questionnaires, tests and quizzes, inventory sheets, and all kinds of material gleaned from recovery books. After working as a clerk for a while, something started to happen: I started taking the program more seriously. I actually started thinking about possibly remaining permanently clean after my release.

Recovery for me started when I was a clerk in Project Change. Like me, most addicts are human garbage cans when it comes to chemical substances. Achieving recovery without any help from rehabs, self-help groups, or counseling is a pyrrhic victory over addiction, which is referred to as a process of natural recovery, also known as spontaneous remission in the medical profession. I don't recommend it.

Spontaneous remission from drug addiction is something that is not ac-knowledged much in addiction/recovery literature. Although I had Project Change and NA to bolster my emerging recovery, those who would rather strike out on their own to recover, could try some of the creativity that I employed in the joint. This process could be thought of as a spontaneous remission if there were no outside forces influencing those who use it. Or, it can be used concomitantly with other methods of recovery, like the one I outline in this book, which I do recommend.

It occurred to me in prison that if I was going to remain clean when I hit the streets, I needed to change my thinking. As it was, I spent every waking hour either thinking about the bar I used to work in, the people I drank and used with, and the women I slept with. I learned in Project Change that if intrinsic and lasting change is going to take place for jointsters like me, they need to monitor and discipline their thought processes.

That made a lot of sense to me, so I decided to literally shoo those old thoughts away, and replace them with different thoughts, more productive ones. I say literally, because with my hand moving in a swooshing motion by my ear, I shooed those thoughts away. Walking around the big yard shooing thoughts away in that manner, I could tell by the looks I was getting that I was being viewed through jaundiced eyes. *Look at that freak*, they must have thought. I didn't care what they thought. I'd never see any of them again anyway once I was released.

At first it took me a long time to remember to shoo those ever-present thoughts away, so I only did the swooshing thing two or maybe three times a day at first--whenever I'd think of it. As time passed, I started remembering more often and doing it more, and more, until I was doing it a lot. That's when I started getting so many of *the looks* from my fellow jointsters. After awhile I discovered that I wasn't doing it as often. Day by day I did it less and less. And then guess what? After about two or three months, I completely exorcized those thoughts from my mind and replaced them with thoughts of what I really wanted to be doing when I was released.

I visualized myself in NA meetings and college classrooms. I also visualized taking care of my aged and ailing mother. Upon my release, I did those things and more. And thanks to Kathy, a teacher in the Project Change program who took a special interest in my academic ability. She nagged me until I agreed to enroll in college. Then she helped me fill out all of those tedious financial aide forms. When I was released, I was already enrolled in college. All I had to do was register for classes when the new semester started.

Participation mystique is a term coined by Lévy-Bruhl. It denotes a peculiar kind of psychological connection with people, and consists in the fact that people can't clearly distinguish themselves from other people but is bound to them by a direct relationship which amounts to partial identity.

Facets of personality can be described as a participation mystique. Highly successful people may routinely step outside of these confines to accomplish what they wish. Participation mystique is a type of mental conditioning that causes people to create and operate within mental boundaries. Such boundaries create an unfounded sense of security. Like inertia, those who have fallen into this trap in a particular area of their lives, will tend to stay trapped without stepping outside of it. To step outside of the trap, they must experiment with new and different behaviors, and then experience the new and different responses that then occur within their environment. This is what addicts need to do with their thinking.

All Addicts are caught in this trap when they don't want to cut loose their old friends, places, and things. After first getting clean, I relapsed three times because I continued to go around my old using friends periodically. Participation mystique is recognizable in other aspects of an addict's character, such as the being-cool thing. With me, being cool started in junior high school in the fifties with duck tails, wearing taps on our shoes, customizing our Levis, and wearing them down so low that the cracks of our asses were showing. This reminds me of a funny story from back then.

Two of my friends at that time were caught breaking windows in homestead shacks that used to be so ubiquitous in the Barstow area. The police cut them loose to their parents, but that wasn't the end of it. Their parents, who were sisters, agreed that their punishment would be for them to wear their pants up high for two weeks. If they were caught cheating, the punishment would get worse. That's how necessary it was for those of us, who thought of ourselves as cool, to wear our Levis that way. We *had* to be cool. At the same time the emerging rock and roll music and James Dean type movies were also influencing us.

Participation mystique also applies to womanizing and manizing (if there is such a word). It's another trap that addicts can fall into. It's the *puer aeternus* personified who flit in and out of romantic relationships. The negative pole of the *puer* is characterized by a poor adjustment to daily demands, a failure to set realistic goals and to make lasting achievements in accord with these goals. Conversational styles are also a part of the participation mystique, and so is rebellion–that anti authority attitude. I carried that attitude with me throughout my 30 years of addiction. The clothes that most addicts wear, as well as their thinking patterns are also inclusive. The ethos of a drug culture is always visible to those in the culture, but not always to those outside of it. Sometimes addicts are forced to be more subtle. Any way we look at it, addicts need to step out of their participation mystique and change, and in order to accomplish that, their thinking needs to change.

To be sure, my alchemical approach to recovery is a model for those who take issue with 12-step programs and/or other types of recovery models. An addict doesn't need to be a member to benefit from meetings. Take me for example. After my release from prison in December 1989, I attended meetings, but I didn't share, I didn't use a sponsor, I didn't and still don't have a higher power, I don't believe in the disease concept, and I don't agree with much of the literature. I do believe, however, that meetings contributed significantly to my recovery because of making new friends and having a social outlet with people I could identify with.

As a student in college, whenever I was given an assignment, I'd try to determine the value of the assignment, and then actually try to learn something from it. I'd even go so far as to try to figure out why the instructor gave the assignment. Many of my fellow students were doing the assignments simply for the sake of the assignment, not for the sake of learning. I also found this practice going on when I was a college and university instructor. It's not difficult to observe the work of a student, and then determine whether the student is just fulfilling an assignment, or putting some heart into it and gaining the benefit of what the assignment was given for in the first place. Addicts, therefore, should keep this in mind when doing the following homework. From this point on, an asterisk (or bold text) will denote homework assignments.

* Make a list with a description of the recurring thoughts that intrude on your consciousness the most.

Before going to prison, I was a bartender and my drug of choice at that time was methamphetamine. The bar and all the people that patronized it (especially the women), and tweaking at the dump, were the two most recurring thoughts that I had to replace. There was other drug and alcohol related thoughts too, of course, but the bar and the dump were the most intrusive. Thought discipline was one of the biggest challenges I've ever had, before or since, and that includes all the challenges I had during 14 years of higher education.

* Immediately start shooing away thoughts and replace them with more opportunistic thoughts, ones that are conducive to recovery.

My method of using a swooshing motion with my hand isn't necessary. By snapping a rubber band around the wrist when old thoughts occur will also work. Partisans can get creative with this. It doesn't matter how they stop their recurring thoughts, as long as they stay at it every waking hour. Thought discipline is crucial. Without it, success is precarious.

≈ II ≈

STAGE TWO

PROBLEM RECOGNITION, AND THE FIRST CONIUNCTIO

Those in the helping professions experienced in working with addicts agree that denial is one of the most difficult problem they encounter. It's also a major reason why many mental health professionals prefer to avoid working with addicts.

Psychologically, denial is an unconscious defense mechanism that is necessary for survival. People can't survive without a certain amount of denial. To protect ourselves, we resort to mechanisms of defense, which are a normal part of our developmental process. Originally conceptualized by Sigmund Freud and later developed by his daughter, Anna Freud, and others, defense mechanisms are unconsciously used by everyone to reduce anxiety when identity is threatened. On the other hand, denial in addicts is taken to extremes and becomes unhealthy in such a way that it becomes an obstacle to recovery.

Why do people in general deny they need help when those around them can see the benefit that professional help could provide? There are many reasons for this. One reason is that people don't like feeling helpless and out-of-control, and this is particularly true with addicts. Addicts will blame everything and anyone except their own drug or alcohol use for their problems. Another reason is that addicts may be using chemical substances to mask or numb undesirable feelings.

As tolerance and loss of control increase and leads to consequences not intended, the identity of addicts begins to shatter. They must assure themselves as well as others that drugs and alcohol are *not* a problem, although the addicted tissue structure of the body makes increasing demands. One way to comprehend the power of drugs is to imagine that body cells are screaming for them and that this demand takes precedence over and rules the mind. The mind assures itself that what's happening isn't happening at all. Toxicity overcomes the rational mind and replaces it with the drug-induced belief that there's not a problem.

The strength of the denial isn't the same in everybody. It varies from addict to addict, and within the same addict, according to life situations and mental health, as well as what stage of addiction they're in. For those in the early stage who have sufficient awareness and have retained some stability, there is greater availability to consider the effect of their chemical indulgences. At the opposite extreme is the addict with little to lose, for whom chemicals makes a wretched life more bearable. This wretchedness can be the result of life traumas.

Not all addicts have suffered traumas in their lives, but an inordinate amount has. Sexual and physical abuse as children is common with addicts as are other kinds of trauma such as rape, wartime experiences, or violent crime. Addicts may be using substances to anesthesize the uncomfortable feelings from post-traumatic stress disorder (PTSD), caused from past traumas, which will eventually need to be dealt with in order for full recovery to occur.

It doesn't matter what the cause of denial is. What's necessary is for addicts to confront this defense mechanism head on. This may be what's commonly known as *hitting bottom*, or can come from confrontation with family, friends, employers, or through court systems. Often addicts will lose jobs, friends, or family relationships because of their addiction and start to face the denial because their lives have actually become so troublesome that they're uncomfortable in their own skin.

Denial with addicts is not a linear course either. They might be in denial sometimes, and face reality at others, so addicts who are in denial may be adaptable, especially in the beginning stages of recovery. Even for those who are far along in recovery, falling off the wagon and being in denial can occur at any time, and needs to be overcome *again* to get back on track. A habit is indeed a malady for which one needs to take responsibility in order to break free.

Those beginning the recovery process must recognize how drugs and/or alcohol is effecting their lives. Symbolically, this is being in the state of *nigredo*–the blackening of the alchemical vessel. Eventually addicts need to determine whether they are in recovery for intrinsic or extrinsic purposes. If addicts are seeking recovery because of a nudge from the judge, to get their spouses back, to save their jobs, or for any other *extrinsic* purpose, then they will probably be forced to admit that a successful recovery is very unlikely. Recovery is usually temporary until they start seeking recovery for themselves.

Homework assignments are important, even though they might not seem so at the time. These assignments are tools that enable recovering addicts to evaluate their lives. Most addicts don't know themselves as well as they like to think they do, so it's imperative that they are uncompromisingly honest. They should spend at least an hour a day on these assignments. After each of the following assignments, I'll give examples from my own life like I did at the end of the preceding chapter.

As stated in the previous chapter concerning alchemy, the mercurial spirit of the prima materia is otherwise known as chaos, and those entering the recovery process definitely fit that description. It is the job of the alchemist to kill the prima materia and in the process the prima materia turns into the blackening state of nigredo. This sets the stage for a transformation--the first coniunctio.

The first coniunctio begins when the ego (consciousness) discovers the reality of the unconscious psyche and makes an effort to pay attention to it. If recovery is being sought for intrinsic purposes, then the ego has acknowledged an unconscious need; therefore, the first coniunctio is the transformation from the dregs of active addiction to the *clamor* of abstinence (again, I emphasize clamor because early abstinence is often as chaotic as active addiction). This part of the transformation is tentative and unstable, and the most susceptible for relapse; therefore, some type of rite of passage should occur at this point.

Sometimes addicts stay clean and sober for a period of time to prove they can stop anytime they want. They can then start drinking or using again because they have *proved* there is no need to quit. Whenever addicts do this, they're obviously *not* in recovery.

Homework Assignments

As an instructor, one of the most common problems I found with students at the undergraduate level is that many of them didn't pay close enough attention to the syllabus. Because of this inattention, they didn't follow the directions the way they were written, and then they wondered why they didn't receive the grades they expected. There's no grading here, but it is essential for partisans to do these assignments as they're written. Spend at least one to two hours a day on assignments. Longer if there isn't many time constraints.

* Do something for the first coniunctio.

My friend Rich wrote a dear John letter to alcohol. Alcohol being his drug of choice, he wrote the letter as though alcohol were a lover that he was giving up. It was a letter that he put a lot of time and effort into, about eight to 10 handwritten pages. In early recovery, I went through a Hazeldon work book. Rich's dear John letter and my workbook are both analogous to the first coniunctio. Those are just two examples. Partisans can choose any method they like, so long as it's momentous and meaningful, something that really establishes a major transition. This rite of passage doesn't need to be as monumental as the second coniunctio, but it should be enough to leave an indelible psychological impression in the psyche of addicts who are serious about their recovery.

* Have you seriously damaged or destroyed relationships with friends because of your addiction? If you have, write down those relationships and how you damaged them.

During my addiction to meth, I was stranded in a rural community about four miles from where I lived. I went to a friend's house nearby to ask for a ride, but there wasn't anyone home. The door was open so I went in, initially just to cool off. Once I was comfortable, I started looking around. By the time I'd left, I'd filled up a backpack, a backpack (I might add) that I found in the house, with items that didn't belong to me.

Someone saw me leave the house and told my friend. When he confronted me about it, I denied it. I could tell he didn't believe me, and because of it, both him and his wife would have nothing to do with me from then on.

If you've been told by others how you've hurt them, put it on paper.

My third wife got a traffic citation when we lived in Las Vegas. I bought drugs with the money that was supposed to be for her fine, so she had to get a continuance. I did it again, and she was granted another continuance. I spent the money yet again, but this time I bought a beautiful picture for our house with the money. She wouldn't go to court this time unless I went with her. When the judge asked if she could pay the fine, she said, "No, your honor, I can't!" and then she turned around and pointed her finger directly at me and said, "because he spent the money on a picture of a naked woman." Many spectators in the court room started laughing, and even the judge was incapable of repressing a smile. He gave her another continuance and I finally paid the fine. However, I put my poor wife through hell and she often reminded me of it.

* Write down how and when you have damaged or destroyed relationships with your loved ones in order to indulge in your addiction.

I had three wives, two of which were common law. Because of my daily drug and alcohol consumption, and my continual association with friends, I was not a very good spouse. I was away from home most of the time, and when I was home, I wasn't really with them. I was still with my friends. In fact, I usually had a friend living with us. Two of these women had extra-marital affairs and they all left because of my chemical indulgences and lack of spousal obligations.

My first wife and I had a daughter which I ended up raising with the help of the other two wives and occasional girlfriends. My daughter ended up in Alcoholics Anonymous when she was 18. She did a thorough fifth step on me, and has since forgiven me for everything I'd put her through. It wasn't easy being raised by a jointster like me.

* Write down any illnesses that your addiction has caused.

I was an intravenous drug user. As with most jointsters who've used drugs this way, I have hepatitis C. I can't be sure why I don't have symptoms with such a high viral count, but my best guess, and my primary care physician agrees, that it's because of healthy eating habits, ingesting various vitamin and mineral supplements, and especially a rigorous exercise program, which I'm easily able to do with the full-blown gym I have in my home.

All of this, I believe, has strengthened my immune system that's enabled me to fight off symptoms. The vast majority who have hep c aren't as lucky, and they are the ones with the more common type 1 genotype.

I don't know why I ended up with type 2, but I often wonder if it's because I have the rarest blood type there is–AB negative. Many of my friends have either died from hep C or have gone through the miserable interferon treatments. One of them went through the treatment twice and still died. Those who used drugs intravenously should immediately get tested, because even if they only used a needle once and it was twenty years ago, they should assume they have the virus.

* Write down occasions when you expressed anger toward others.
While driving drunk with my five-year-old daughter in the car, some driver made an error in judgment and through circumstances of the incident, I ended up blocking him with my car. I got out of the car and opened his door and jerked him out of the car. I started to hit him but he acted scared, so in a moment of clarity, probably resulting from knowing that my daughter was watching, I let him go and returned to my car. I'm grateful that my daughter doesn't remember the incident, but there are many more incidents that she does remember and I don't.

* Write down incidents in your life related to your addiction that caused you to be embarrassed or humiliated.
I have 40 recorded arrests on my police record, so it pretty much goes without saying that there were embarrassment and humiliation during many of those usually very public arrests, but what comes to mind is different from that. When living in Las Vegas, I was receiving Aid for Dependent Children (welfare). Personal hygiene wasn't one of my strongest suits, but I wasn't usually embarrassed by it, that is until I had to go in for an interview at the ADC office. The social worker unhesitatingly told me that I smelled bad, and that I should either bathe or wash my clothes more often. I didn't want to be terminated from the program, so I held back when I wanted to lash out verbally. As with most addicts, embarrassment or humiliation usually turns to anger.

* Put in writing any times in the past that you tried to *control* your addiction, and mention how successful or unsuccessful each time was.
For about nine years, I wrote and called in my own medical prescriptions for pharmaceutical opiates. Tussionex, at the time (the formula has since been changed), was highly addictive. Sometimes I'd get tired of the chase and the periodic arrests by the law, so I'd quit. That is I'd quit Tussionex. I still wrote scrips for other opiates like Percodan and Tylenol w Codeine, so I wasn't really quitting, was I?

   To demonstrate how early psychological addiction can set in, my first attempt on the water wagon occurred when I was 15 years old. I told myself that I wasn't going to drink anymore. The very next time my friends offered me some beer or wine, I accepted, and quitting was something I didn't even attempt again for many years.

* Are you sorry for the ways that you have acted during your addiction? If you are, put it on paper. Write at least three ways.
My 13-year-old daughter and I went to the grocery store to pick up a few items. I was holding the items in my arms while waiting in line. I got angry because the store didn't have enough checkers. The longer we stood there, the angrier I became. Finally, I threw all the items in the air and said, "C'mon Snivels, let's get outta here," then I yelled some obscenity about the store and stormed out. I'm still sorry for that, but I probably wouldn't have been sorry had my

daughter not told me years later how much that incident embarrassed her. At the time it didn't even occur to me that she was embarrassed, and if it did I doubt if I'd given a shit.

My drug of choice was meth during the last four or five years of my addiction. During that time a friend asked if I knew anyone who would beat up someone for her. She offered a hundred dollars. I said I'd check around. One of my drug connections said he'd do it, so I got the hundred dollars from her and gave it to him. He kept the hundred dollars and didn't do what he was paid to do, so I felt obligated to give back her money (I didn't want her hiring someone to beat me up). At the time, my mom kept a stash of money under the cushion of an old chair in her bedroom, so the next time she left the house, I stole a hundred dollars and paid the money back to my friend. My mom never missed the money and I never paid it back, but I've been sorry about it ever since.

* Write down any irrational or crazy set of events that have happened since you began your addiction. If you rationalized this behavior, write down how.
The last of the five formal terms of probations that I served, I convinced myself that my probation officer (PO) wouldn't test me--this time. I convinced myself of this so I wouldn't have to go three days without drugs to clean out my system. Rarely did he not test me, so my thinking was grossly irrational. Usually, when he'd ask if I'd been using, I'd admit it, which is why I got away with so many dirty tests. Evidently, he appreciated the honesty. Most addicts will deny having used anything. At least that way, jail would be postponed until the test results came back. Of course, I learned this the hard way.

* Put in writing how you have avoided others because they disapproved of your addiction. Also include who they were and the circumstances.
Most partisans will say that they've avoided people who disapproved of their addiction. That's what I said because I chose to associate only with people who used drugs and/or alcohol. However, I didn't think I could avoid having girlfriends. I'd lie by telling them I had something pressing to do when I'd previously committed myself to something else with them. Scenarios such as this are common among addicts.

When I first started using, I still had several friends who didn't use. If I was with my friends that used, and we encountered a friend who didn't, we'd give him some excuse why he couldn't come with us. At that early stage of my addiction, I'd feel sorry for my non using friend when that happened. That type of guilt didn't last long, however, and eventually they didn't even want to come with us because our reputations had deteriorated so much.

* Pinpoint on paper exactly when your life started to deteriorate, and what was going on in your life at that time.
I started drinking at twelve years old, but only on weekends. The summer of my 15th year, I got my first DUI on my Cushman motor scooter. I was jailed

three times that summer. I was still in high school, and going to jail at that time in my life was looked at by my peers as cool. It wasn't very cool to my dad, however, and he took my scooter away to prove it.

* Write down exactly what made you realize that you had a problem, and why you couldn't control it.
As I stated earlier, I realized I had a drinking problem when I was 15. Nor did it take me long to realize that drugs were a problem after a couple years of using. My drug and alcohol use lasted 30 years, but it wasn't until my prison experience that I realized that my drug and alcohol consumption was impossible to control.

Addicts using this self-help method of recovery really need to know how much work it's going to be and how long it's going to take.

≈ III ≈

STAGE THREE

A RECKONING

Stage three is a personal history and a reckoning. This history should include not only the deep dark immoral secrets of hedonistic and scandalous turpitude, but also the more admirable traits that have often gone unnoticed.

Recovering from a life of chaos caused by the rigors of addiction is what most addicts would like to achieve, but most of them don't have the wherewithal to accomplish. I believe in a process. This process, you might say, is the brainchild of another book I've written about my life, but this process is not a new idea. Books and articles have been written about journaling, and it's a tool used by many counselors to enhance the lives of their clients. Socrates said that an unexamined life is not worth living.

Writing a history of one's life can and often does serve as an impetus for recovery. It'll also serve as a map into the territory we call experience and memory, showing where we and others have traveled, and leading into areas of human experience that are so essential to this odyssey we call life. I expect, as the process has for me, that along the way many others can or will uncover lost and forgotten pieces of themselves, and in the process they might discover hidden places within their souls that are springs of healing and the discovery of a life yet unlived.

Like a compass, a life history points in only one direction. If addicts who start the process of writing their history are anything like me, they'll want to make what's left of their lives more meaningful than their past. All they have to do is take the first step. Once this journey is embarked upon, change, to some degree, is inevitable and the writer's could in unexpected ways feel themselves changing into different people.

In antiquity Heraclitus said that you can never step into the same river twice. This wisdom exemplifies the flowing nature of reality. This morning when I woke up I looked at the same walls in my house, same kitchen, same living room, same everything. It's all the same at first glance, but is it? Today is a brand-new day. This moment is a new moment and one that's never been lived. I am a day older and the world is constantly evolving and changing. Life is like a river and every moment is different. I realize these words sound a bit lofty, but it's hard to deny their significance.

Writing a life history may be one of the most personal and intimate processes addicts can do. Through their personal history, they can come to know who they are in new and unforeseen ways. They can also reveal to others what's deepest in their hearts, and in the process build bridges instead of destroying them. The very act of sharing a personal history contradicts the isolation that characterizes the lives of so many addicts. A life history carries within it the seeds of the environment, and because life histories take time and patience to write, they can serve as potent antidotes to depression, self-loathing, and demoralization, which is so common among addicts. Without a past, we have no place to stand, no place from which to see, and no clear direction for our future.

A life history for addicts becomes the vehicle through which they organize the events that happen to them. It's also a way of telling time. A life history takes shape like chapters in a book, each in its proper place, one following the next, explaining why events happened as they did, lending logic to decisions and bringing meaning to what would otherwise be a collection of drunkalogues or drugalogues. Without life histories, life becomes a book cover without the pages—nice to look at, but not very meaningful.

At the end of our lives, all that's left are our histories. In a unique and fascinating way, these life histories are our tickets to immortality. Knowing that future generations will read and retell our stories, and knowing that other recovering addicts will read and be inspired by them, makes it a worthwhile and gratifying effort

Starting such a project can be daunting, however, so the best way to proceed is to incorporate what I refer to as automatic writing. That is, just start writing, whether there's a plan in mind or not. Write something, anything, just to get started, and keep writing for thirty minutes. It doesn't matter whether the words makes sense, whether the ramblings are grammatically correct, or whether there are misspelled words. Just keep writing without stopping, not even for two seconds. Once there's a chunk of text visible, the beginning of a life history, which could end up in the form of a book, has been started. It can be edited later.

In the beginning, it was hard for an addict like me to gather memories that were obliterated from so many years of addiction, so I used my police record as a guide. My arrest record spans 30 years and I have three different copies of it—one from the sixties, one from the eighties, and a recent one. Another device that helped was my employment record from the Social Security Administration. With those tools, I was surprised how much I started re-membering. I also dug into the memories of my old friends who shared some of my experiences.

If we could open up the mind like the hood of a car, the task would be much simpler. While experience is encoded by all the senses, the primary fuel that triggers memory is often pictorial. However, there are exceptions. I, for one, think in words, but many people rely on other senses for their perspectives of the world. Regardless of a person's learning orientation, research confirms that for most people, it's the *image* of past events that are most accessible to recollection, whether that image is pictorial or rhetorical.

Each time we journey inward and trace the path of a memory to its origins, we seem to discover nuances and connections that were previously unnoticed. The illumination of our current awareness is also conditioned by our emotional state and by seemingly trivial matters such as the aroma of a former lover or the sound of familiar music, thereby filtering the process of recall. For example, the smell of a used book store could open a door to a whole realm of past experience that I haven't considered for years. I might see myself standing next door to an old book store with a friend I haven't thought of for a long time. An old girlfriend's beautiful face suddenly intrudes on this memory. Her touch changes into my favorite aunt's hand patting me on the head. My mind wanders through a multitude of images and warm feelings (or perhaps cold ones). With addicts, there are often as many, if not more, negative feelings coming over them as the warm ones. Whatever the feelings and images are, they are the fuel, the words needed for a life history.

With Partisans allowing themselves to be purposefully drawn inward, something remarkable happens. Their past merges with the present, permitting them to reclaim and recreate something formerly hidden. Moving against the tide of the present, however, requires a conscious decision, an act of will to re-member. If addicts can get half as compulsive with this endeavor as they did with their addiction, perhaps a book could come of it.

Write down the broken relationships with the opposite sex, and explain how those broken relationships hurt them and/or you. Note any anger or resentments concerning these relationships.

In the life history I wrote, I made a thorough account concerning my three wives and the pain and anguish I caused them. For example, my second wife was my daughter's first step mom. When she left me for another man, I did everything I could think of to inject her with a heavy dose of depression for running out on us. I told her how devastated my daughter was, which wasn't really true, because my daughter was so young, and Jackie and I wasn't together all that long. I was saying anything I could think of to get her back. I was successful, not in getting her back, but injecting a heavy dose of depression in her. I learned later that she ended up in therapy, mainly because of the loss of my daughter whom she really did come to love. The loss of me was minimal because she wanted out of the relationship quite a while before she left.

The anger and resentment I held on to for so long, of course, came after the broken heart. In front of my friends, however, I told a different story. "Fuck that bitch, I'm glad she's gone. I should've gotten rid of her sooner." Bullshsit! That's the inflated male ego which is so prevalent among primarily male addicts.

Write down when you have acted self-righteously, and whether you believed you were justified and why.

Also prevalent in the drug culture is criminalization, where lying and stealing is ubiquitous. Some of my friends and I thought we were exceptions because we didn't lie to or steal from each other. We didn't have a problem with stealing from employers, stores, and any company or organization that we thought could afford the loss. When meth became popular, I and my click of friends fell into the trap of feeling self-righteous. We thought we were better than the majority of speed freaks who had no qualms about stealing from friends, family, or whoever else crossed their paths. Most addicts are saddled with a syndrome, and that is an inflated ego coupled with low self-esteem. They know that most normies think of them as scumbags, and it certainly isn't uncommon for addicts to think of themselves that way either, but rarely do they admit it. Self-righteousness scumbags. How's that for an oxymoron?

Put in writing what influenced your addictive behavior.
Most people separate alcoholism from drug addiction, workaholism, sex addiction, gambling, and overeating, etc. With that in mind, I'll proceed with a short discussion on addictive behavior. Does the addictive behavior of parents teach their offspring addictive behavior? Is addictive behavior physiologically determined or genetic? Has society, through the media, contributed its share of the blame? Is peer pressure to blame? Is addictive behavior a result of inadequate coping mechanisms? Are addicts solely responsible for their own actions and behavior? Or, is it a combination of these, and more. Most scholars in the field agree that it is a combination. Some researchers emphasize some over others. It's my contention that there are *more* causes and dynamics going on than what's stated above or in the literature.

Addictive behavior in parents often begets addictive behavior in their offspring. If a child grows up in a family in which one parent is an addict, the child is likely to develop an addiction. If both parents are addicts, the child's chances of addiction increase. Subsequently, the generational cycle of addiction continues. When adult children of addicts seek relationships, it is usually with people who are similar to them. This search doesn't usually happen on a conscious level. It is what Freud called repetition compulsion.

It has been argued that the tendency toward addiction is biological, inherited genetically, or a result of chemical imbalances. Will diagnoses like hypoendorphism or opioid receptor insufficiency or hypodopaminosis ever be made with reliability? I wouldn't count on it.

Heredity isn't as simple as what was previously believed. At conception, we receive a unique set of genetic material--internal instructions that guide growth and development. These instructions set limits in the form of predispositions. The outcome will depend on unique life circumstances and the environment. Researchers who claim that there's a genetic predisposition for weight also suggest that there is a genetic predisposition for addiction. How can we really know? The best that science can come up with is based on probability. Combined with life circumstances, addiction is likely, which is giving credence to nature *and* nurture rather than nature *or* nurture. To complicate matters, the media among other causal factors, contributes its share of influence.

No one escapes the media's power to promote excess. Big business sells both gluttony and dieting, smoking, eroticism and an exaggerated need for the work ethic. Television commercials convey messages to addict its audience. The commercial of a lady who puts her hand to her pain-wrinkled forehead and complains "Oh, this terrible headache," is generally seen in the next scene chipper and happy, thanking a miraculous wonder drug. Billboards with the Marlboro Man or Joe Camel have done their part in influencing us. Other influential media, directed at youth, is the glamorization of reckless lifestyles in movies. Kids grow up in a sea of advertising. Pre- adolescents see and hear beer and wine ads and commercials exhorting them to drink before they're old enough. It can hardly be denied that the overall effect of advertisements is to glamorize whatever it is being sold, whether it's cigarettes, alcohol, or over-the-counter medication, and to encourage the idea that what is being advertised will make them feel better or enhance their lives in some way.

It appears that life events may be mediating factors in the development of mental and emotional illnesses in general, and drug abuse in particular. What if dad's brother died? What if dad lost his job? What if dad had to serve a jail sentence? What if mom was an only child, not having the large-family experience, and then grew up and had five children? What if she was a full-time housewife, belonged to the PTA, held a part-time job, and was expected to participate in civic activities? Could addiction be a coping mechanism for life events such as dad's, and stress such as mom's? Researchers reported that within a group of alcoholic and nonalcoholics, the alcoholic group reported the impact of stress to a higher level than the nonalcoholic group. These results can apply to pre alcoholic men and women too, creating a need to relieve stress. "It calms me down. It helps my nerves. It helps me unwind after a hard day." These comments can be viewed as *anxiety thesis*. Partially a derivative of Freud's work, he stated that during times of anxiety and stress, people look to the past for things that worked for them.

During puberty and early adolescence there is a need for identity. Young people want to break from their parents. They fall into close associations with peers, and those peers have a profound influence. Peer pressure can also come from the workplace. Adolescent and occupational research both suggest that drinking is a learned behavior, and that it is learned from those who have the most social influence. To be included in certain subcultures, it is necessary to drink or use drugs.

People who develop drug and alcohol related problems later in life are likely to have started using drugs and alcohol at an earlier age than is typical for the general population. Also, the presence of heavy drinking and drug-using partners has been found to increase both the amount and rate at which substances are consumed.

These theories, et al, are what the prevailing literature proposes as causes and conditions of addiction. Physical addiction, especially in the early stages, isn't physical when applied to substance abusers in general, because most people who are thought of as addicts are not physically addicted, as heroin addicts are. Most of them have what I've termed an *addictive mind-set and lifestyle*. When I tried to quit drinking when I was 15 years old, it was my psychological addiction coupled with peer influence that rendered me unsuc-cessful.

Stress, as discussed above, is an anomaly with many addicts. To get an idea what a addict's stress level is, here is a stress test. Check each item that has happened in the last year, then add up the points.

Marriage (53)
Troubles with your boss (23)
Detention in jail or other institution (63)
Death of Spouse (100)
Major change in sleeping habits (16)
Death of a close family member (63)
Major change in eating habits (15)
Foreclosure on a mortgage or loan (30)
Revision of personal habits - dress, manners, associations, etc (24)
Death of a close friend (37)
Minor violation of the law (11)
Outstanding Personal Achievement (28)
Pregnancy (40)
Major change in the health or behavior of a family member (44)
Sexual difficulties (39)
In-law troubles (29)
Major change in number of family get-togethers (15)
Major change in financial status (38)
Gaining a new family member (39)
Change in residence (20)
Son or daughter leaving home (29)
Marital separation from mate (63)
Major change in church activities (19)
Marital reconciliation with mate (47)
Being fired from work (50)
Divorce (73)
Changing to a different line of work (36)
Major change in the number of arguments with spouse (35)
Major changes in responsibilities at work (29)
Spouse beginning or ceasing work outside the home (26)
Major change in working hours or conditions (20)
Major change in usual type and/or amount of recreation (19)
Taking on a mortgage or loan greater than $10,000. (31)
Taking on a mortgage or loan less than $10,000. (17)
Major personal injury or illness (63)
Major business readjustment (39)
Major change in social activities (18)
Major change in living conditions (25)
Retirement from work (45)
Vacation (13)
Christmas (12)
Changing to a new school (20)
Beginning or ceasing formal schooling (26)

Scoring:
150 - 299 means a 33% chance of illness or accident in the next year.
300 - 499 means a 66% chance of illness or accident in the next year.
450 + means a 90% chance of an illness or accident in the next year.

Write down specific situations, emotions, experiences, and the people you associated with before your addictive mind-set and lifestyle began.
I had a happy childhood. When reflecting on *when* the seeds of drug and alcohol use and criminality was planted in my young mind, I am reminded of the time when I was about eight years old, when I picked a flower off someone's bush as I walked down the sidewalk. I turned around and noticed a police car coming around the corner. Immediately, I took off running. I ran up to my friend's door and banged on it. When he answered, I quickly went inside, turned around, looked down the street, then closed the door and said emphatically, "The cops are after me!" Something attracted me to a lifestyle characteristic of the behavior I was acting out. Did I *really* think the cops were after me? Probably not. Did I want my friend to think the cops were after me? Probably.

Write down all the grudges you held and if you got revenge, and include whether or not anyone was hurt.
When I lived in Las Vegas, I had a 56 Buick that I was driving temporarily for my window cleaning business when my work car was out of service. The trunk didn't lock when it was closed like most cars. One day I had a friend of a friend helping me clean windows. I had a large jar of pennies in the trunk. The next day when I got into the trunk, the pennies were gone. I didn't hold a grudge for long. A day or two later, I drove by his house and shot a couple of 22 bullets through the front window of his home. I never learned whether anyone was hurt, and I never saw or heard from him again. Last I heard, he was in prison. I knew he had a wife and child before I did it, but I did it anyway. If anyone was hurt, I'm glad now that I didn't find out.

Put on paper what you hate most in others, and whether you have any of these traits?
This will be difficult for most addicts to do. I don't believe I'm alone when I get annoyed by people who constantly talk about themselves. These people will immediately turn the conversation back to themselves if someone else changes the subject. Fortunately, I've trained myself to not do that anymore, but there was a time when I did, and that was during my years of heavy alcohol consumption. We bring a lot of psychological baggage with us into recovery and it takes a real effort to change, and change is what recovery is all about.

There are times when I've witnessed someone doing or saying something inappropriate to someone else. It not being my place to say anything, I think to myself that the person being disrespected should say or do something about it. It's a negative judgement call. What I came to learn about myself, is that I have been guilty of the same thing on more occasions than I'd like to admit.

Document the damage you've done to loved ones, and how you have or are going to make up for it. Be specific and discuss them all.

I loved my parents, but I sometimes wonder how I could've done much of what I did after they'd been so consistently good to me. One night when I was around 17 years old, I sneaked my parent's car out and went out drinking and smoking pot with my friends. We went to a spot in the desert. Driving up the old canyon road, I ran over a big rock or up the side of a hill, and the car went over on its side. The damage wasn't all that bad, so we pushed it back onto its wheels. Amazingly, it started up, so I parked and we did what we went there to do. When we finished with our pot and beer, I took them home and returned the car to its parking space.

My mom was a periodic alcoholic, and on this particular weekend she'd been tying one on with her brother. The next morning my dad came into my room and asked, "What happened to the Corvair?"

"What do you mean?" I replied innocently.

"Well, it looks like it was tipped over on its side."

As if I didn't know what he was talking about, I said, "I don't know, let's see." We walked outside and looked it over. After looking at it, I shook my head a little and said, "Dad," and then motioning toward the house with my head, I said, "she's been drinking all weekend. Maybe you should ask her."

I don't know what transpired between my parents, and my dad never mentioned the incident again, but several years later I asked my mom about it. She said that she told him she couldn't remember damaging the car, but that it was possible. I believe that's what she told him, but she probably said it in such a defiant way that further conversation about the incident would've been fruitless and ugly. The bottom line was that she managed to cover my ass without admitting to anything. I was under the impression that my dad couldn't be sure which of us did it, so he treated us both indifferently for a while. Eventually he forgot about it. Needless to say, my mother really loved me, and she went on proving it in many ways for the rest of her life, especially when it came to protecting me.

What I did was despicable. Why would I do that to my mother? How did I live with myself afterwards without the least bit of remorse? And why do so many parents put up with such reprehensible behavior?

To begin with, I didn't do what I did *to* my mother. I was defending myself. My age and my growing defiance and self-centeredness enhanced by my growing dependence on chemical substances, made me very egocentric. As heartless as it may seem, rather than remorse, I thought I was being hip, slick, and cool by getting away with something, and for many years that was my *modus operandi*: getting away with something, pulling a fast one, getting over, tricking someone, pulling the wool over, a con job. This type of behavior is characteristic of jointsters and I was impressed by it anytime I witnessed it in others.

When I was released from prison, I got to make up for the things I did to my mother by taking care of her until she died. She didn't expect me to make up for anything, and I didn't do it at the time to be making up for anything, but that's the way I'm looking at it now. My dad died when I was 23. I never got to do anything to make up to him. He died believing I was a failure as a son. I imagine he thought himself as a failure too for not being able to steer me in the right direction. I know he would be proud now, but it's a little late.

≈ IV ≈

STAGE FOUR

DIVULGENCE
AND THE SECOND CONIUNCTIO

The practice of divulgence is a very ancient one. For almost 2,000 years it has been a sacramental practice in the Catholic Church. It is an exercise in humility and honesty that characterizes the lives of all spiritually centered and religious people. Some spiritual directors consider it the foundation for any active, profound and meaningful spiritual life.

It has also been a sound therapeutic practice for mental health professionals. It's a cleansing process and the discovery, acknowledgment, admission and discussion of one's life experiences are looked upon as a necessary beginning of the change process.

Most addicts don't have a problem disclosing their nefarious past in prayers or to themselves, but divulging their past with someone other than a cohort, such as what's recommended in 12-step programs, is usually out the question. It's difficult for addicts to trust anyone. In the early stages of recovery, addicts are still learning to trust themselves and hopefully make an attempt to trust others as well.

All of those despicable things that addicts have done during their addiction have been kept a secret and needs to be talked about. If they prefer not to bear their souls to either a counselor, clergy, 12-step sponsor, or psychotherapist, then a friend or acquaintance—clean and sober or not—will suffice. Most friends or acquaintances of addicts have done most of the despicable things that recovering addicts have done, if not worse, so there's really no reason not to divulge a past that they're not proud of.

After having completed all third stage homework, write down what you have come to realize concerning your limitations and capabilities.
When I look back on my *first* life, which is how I refer to my life prior to recovery, it's glaringly obvious that my limitations were inextricably entwined with my addictive mind-set and lifestyle. Once at 18 and again at 20, I attempted college, but was incapable of sustaining the discipline necessary to acclimate to college life. How could I when I was doing drugs every day? Another one of my limitations was my inability to sustain a romantic relation-ship. The opposite sex doesn't fare well playing second fiddle to drugs or alcohol. The needs of addicts *always* come first, even before family and friends.

Many of the assets and capabilities addicts have during recovery, they also had when they were using drugs and/or alcohol. When I lived in Las Vegas and was addicted to Tussionex (a hydrocodone bronchitis preparation) and Port Wine, my house (inside and out) was dirty and cluttered..Later, however, when I was addicted to meth in Barstow, I kept my room in my mom's house full of junk from the dump. Today, my mom is gone, but I still live in the same house, and (inside and out) it is very organized--so organized that my daughter thinks of me as anal retentive or OCD. These proclivities were present during my addiction but they were repressed because of the primacy of my drug and alcohol use. When I got clean, they seemed to come crawling out of the closet of repression.

During my addiction, I was compulsive when it came to chemical substances. Some of us bring compulsiveness, so characteristic of addicts, into our clean and sober lives. When I was released from prison and started my journey to a brand-new life, I started my college career, and again my compulsiveness kicked in. I couldn't stop until I earned a doctorate. Because of my failure in my youth to succeed in college, I accepted the notion that I wasn't college material. I suppose I wasn't then, with such a greedy appetite for drugs and alcohol; therefore it's best for addicts to keep in mind that whatever they were during their addiction, doesn't necessarily apply any more once they've started the recovery process.

Put in writing what divulging the past was like, and what your feelings were before, during, and after the process.

What's the point in addicts divulging to someone all of their misconduct unless there are reasons for doing it? Tao Te Ching once said that those who know others are wise, but those who know themselves are enlightened. The Ancient Greek aphorism "Know thyself," was inscribed in the pronaos (forecourt) of the Temple of Apollo at Delphi according to the Greek periegetic (travelogue) writer Pausanias. Self-knowledge is simply a matter of self- understanding and knowing what makes one tick. Every person is unique and nobody is perfect. The perfect human being hasn't been born yet and never will. A major accomplishment for addicts to achieve is to learn what they're capable of and to know themselves- all their *strengths* and weaknesses. The more they understand themselves, the more powerful their recovery will be.

Life offers so much but so many addicts allow it to drift by without making the slightest effort to reach their full potential. That is wasteful in the extreme because if addicts don't achieve what they're capable of, they and the world around them suffers. A addict's contribution could be vital to the anima mundi (world soul). More on the anima mundi in chapter 10.

Usually by this time, addicts will have witnessed the contents of the alchemical vessel transform from the blackening of the nigredo to the whitening of the albedo. They will discuss with a friend or helpmate at what point of the alchemical process they believe they're in. If they have internalized their recovery thus far as an alchemical process and recognize the importance of the transformation of the second coniunctio, then their journey of transformation can continue uninhibited. Hopefully, by this time, addicts have internalized the death of their old selves and the birth of the new. The benefit of the previous stages, if addicts have been successful, is the completion of the 2nd coniunctio. The whitening of the alchemical vessel has turned red. Addicts are in the rubedo phase, and like the 1st coniunctio, a rite of passage is essential.

If addicts don't believe they're ready for the 2nd coniunctio's rite of passage, then maybe they should evaluate whether this process is for them or not. It's not for everyone. Some people work better with outside help. Recovering on your own is for those who have the self-discipline for self help. Once the 2nd coniunctio's rite of passage *has* been achieved, then addicts should reward themselves with something they enjoy doing. It's important for all people to enjoy life as much as possible.

The Second Coniunctio

To ignore rites of passage or dismiss them as trivial or unnecessary rituals, is as ridiculous as taking a shower to wash away sins. The Stanton Peele Addiction website notes that, of the Jewish people the sociologists interviewed, none had ever had a drinking problem. Investigating all reports by activists in the Jewish community who had announced a growing alcoholism problem, the sociologists couldn't locate one Jewish alcoholic. I'm sure the same is true concerning other chemical substances as well.

Could it be that a bar mitzvah is responsible for this? Perhaps, at least where drugs and alcohol are concerned. However, judging by reports from the Jewish community, they do have other addictions such as overeating and anorexia. According to the National Jewish Press, Ross (April, 1986) reports that there are "seven to 10 thousand Jewish inmates in the United States." Though that number has probably increased since then, it's still a very small percentage of the more than two million Americans that are behind bars today. Under the aegis of the church, could initiatory rites of passage account for the absence of addiction in Jewish culture? If so, what about other cultures?

Mythologist Mircea Eliade states that initiation in the most general sense denotes a body of rites and oral teachings whose purpose is to produce a decisive alteration in the religious and social status of the person to be initiated.

The closest I came to being elevated from a child to something more than a child, was when I left grammar school and entered junior high. With only a short graduation ceremony from the elementary school level, what followed came as a radical social change. In what seems now like an almost overnight transformation, I went from a pleasant grade school boy to an acerbic junior high school rebel without a cause; from playing on the monkey bars to getting drunk at Friday night football games; from wrestling with schoolmates on the playground to gang fights with rival gangs--riotous, no doubt, just like the Germanic berserkers of antiquity; from playing hide-and-seek with girls to whisking them out of the movie theater to kiss and fondle them--not unlike the mythological Theseus carrying off Adriadne; from recess to smoking in the bath rooms during breaks; from evenings home with parents to malicious mischief in the neighborhood with friends. It could be argued that there is a nexus between our malicious mischief, addiction, and the spirit of initiation. My friends and I felt compelled to prove ourselves to each other, so we acted-out an incredible amount of destructive behavior in the process. This seemingly overnight transformation from boy to renegade, was not observed as such by my parents because the changes to them were slow and subtle. It took them awhile before they started noticing changes because I looked and acted like the same boy who was so recently in grade school. They wasn't paying attention.

My elementary school graduation happened at about the same age as the bar mitzvah does in Jewish culture, which is the time of life when psychological and physiological change naturally occurs, so it is the ideal time for a rite of passage. Being unfamiliar with the bar mitzvah and what their ordeals entail, I believe it is safe to assume that there are painstaking lengths gone to for some kind of enduring conversion. Among the Australian Yuin tribe, a young male's first initiation ceremony, comprising the separation from the women and the ordeal by fire, is thus complete. From that night on the novices share only in the life of the *men.*"

Indeed, the elevation to junior high school with its incumbent social status, seemed to suddenly sever an emotional attachment to my parents, and created a different kind of emotional attachment to my newly acquired friends. These friends, I might add, some of whom I kept for more than 30 years, a few of which I still have today. Obviously, that pubescent ceremony was not in any way doing what a rite of passage should.

Considering the Jewish rites of passage, and similar rites in other cultures, I believe my point is well taken that a significant rite of passage is a life-changing event; however, although the most opportune time is at the pubescent stage, it can still occur anytime during human development. The *puer aeternus* (eternal boy) archetype has enabled the partisan to remain in adolescent psychology. A rite of passage needs to occur to elevate the *puer* or *puella* to a maturity that's tantamount to recovery. A chip and a cake are not enough, especially the redundancy of repeating it every year. It will be up to the partisan to come up with rites of passage significant enough to cement an enduring transformation in his or her life, and I suggest incorporating something prodigious.

If there's one aspect of personal growth that addicts are reluctant to embrace, it's the period of uncertainly that shifting to a new way of life requires. During this critical time, addicts don't often see apparent progress or upward mobility, only an anxious feeling of confusion, perplexity, or even impotence, broken periodically by a mysterious calm. The real problem isn't the feeling itself. It's a reaction to a feeling by demanding them to move quickly out of it. Even in traditional cultures, where the roles that people attained in the course of their lives were well defined, it was widely acknowledged that being confused or perplexed was simply a part of the process, that change required a period of walking through some kind of void. Addicts, in our drug infested society, tend to look over their shoulders and see their guilt-ridden shadows pointing a finger at them, and they feel even more frustrated and inadequate than ever. When periods of uncertainly for addicts finally come to an end, most of them have no idea how or why. And not knowing how they escaped from their apathy tends to carry with it a nagging fear that they just might sink back into the abyss again.

The old saying that most people will choose a familiar problem over an unfamiliar solution is much more that an empty cliche. Unconsciously, addicts work hard to maintain a steady state–to avoid letting go of the familiar–even when the familiar is clearly deleterious. The minds of many people, especially addicts, are very much in the business of maintaining a sense of the familiar, like an anal retentive housekeeper who flinches at the thought of someone rearranging things in their living space or office. Their egos put up a strong resistance to any attempt to impose change on them. This is why it's so easy to look at someone else's problem and see the path they need to take, while trudging down our own road to recovery is a struggle of mythic proportions.

Most rites of passage are structured to emphasize the idea that we must release the old sense of self in order for a new identity to materialize and grow. If addicts have a deep understanding of a need to let go, they can use it as a weapon against the fear of transition. Unfortunately, most of them tend to acknowledge the need for letting go only under extreme circumstances, like after someone dies. For what addicts consider lesser matters like changing jobs or moving away, they are much less able to see the need to let go of anything at all. And that has made the task of recovery a lot more difficult than it needs to be. Analogous to this is the following anecdote.

Mumpsimus - Beware of the dread disease:

Mumpsimus is dangerous. It has caused the downfall of more than one dictator, more than one nation, and countless individuals. Mumpsimus is as old as mankind. According to Webster's Dictionary, mumpsimus is an error obstinately clung to. The word comes from the story of an old priest who, for thirty years had conducted services using the word mumpsimus as a substitute for the correct Latin word sumpsimus. One day, when his error was finally pointed out to him, he replied, "I will not change my old mumpsimus for your new sumpsimus. Mumpsimus is blind adherence to a principle or concept. It's a mistake we continue to repeat, even after we know it's a mistake. For example, students who've read about studying techniques, find the logic behind them solid, recognize their value, and yet continue to use their old methods.

Another example: if people are shown that a drug is harmful, that it can cause pain or illness, and yet they continue to use that drug, then they have a case of mumpsimus.

The afflicted student or drug user, knows the old concepts haven't worked very well, yet continues to act as if they did. Mumpsimus is nothing to feel guilty about. It's just a disease.

Most addicts will find the story of mumpsimus believably amusing. This and other blind spots are concomitantly fed by cultural myths, especially the doctrine of positive thinking, which says that with enough determination, we can go out and do anything we set out to do. Like all myths, this one is only somewhat useful. Positive thinking becomes destructive when it turns into dogma. It leads many people to think that change comes, not from letting go of old patterns, but merely from embracing whatever new thing they think they deserve. When that new thing doesn't change their lives, they're more confused than they were before. Taken to an extreme, this type of thinking often causes people to view divorce, illness, addiction, and even death as some kind of personal failure.

Another myth that serves as a stumbling block to the idea of letting go, especially with addicts, is the notion that they can have it all (the myth of unlimited growth). If addicts define having it all as holding down a job and supporting a family, that's good, but if they think they can add new qualities to their lives without releasing old priorities, then they'll be disappointed.

Recovery for addicts, and the rituals that encourage it, consists of the release of old, familiar ways, and the sacrifice of the comfort in things that's familiar– for the possibility of achieving happiness and fulfillment.

Intuition, inspiration, boredom, depression, and anxiety are all signs that something new is emerging in the lives of addicts. Though they may not always want to listen to these taps on the shoulder, rest assured that the messenger will get their attention one way or another, perhaps in the form of health problems, the loss of an intimate relationship, incarceration, or relapse. Just realizing that these feelings may be signs that this stage of the transition process, the second coniunctio, is unfolding will lighten their transformation. Before addicts embark on the second coniunctio's rite of passage, they should keep in mind three things: (1) the attitudes, behaviors, roles, relationships, and possibilities that they're giving up; (2) the nature and direction of their deepest sentiments and passions, all those things they want to align themselves with in the future; and (3) that there will inevitably be a time of aimless emotional wandering as their sense of direction starts to gel.

Addicts need to invest some time in a rite of passage. They could gather up some carefully selected stones, and go out into the woods, desert, or some isolated spot and embed the stones into the ground, with each one representing things they intend on giving up in their lives, such as the roles, behaviors, perspectives, or relationships that are no longer serving them. To make the rite even more meaningful, they could paint the stones in whatever way would best represent what they attribute to each one. A ceremony to go along with this would also be appropriate. Addicts can return to this site every year for as long as they feel the need. When my mom passed away, I drove more than a hundred miles every year to visit her grave. After ten years, I didn't feel the need to continue doing that anymore.

The variety of ways to focus attention on letting go is limitless. Addicts could write down the old patterns they want to give up, and then bury the pieces of paper a hundred miles apart. Using natural objects as tokens of these old patterns, they could toss them into various rivers and/or lakes. To reinforce the idea that even unhealthy behaviors contain energy that can be transformed into something productive, they could carve a chunk of wood to represent an old habit or behavior, and then carve other ones to represent other old habits or behaviors. Or, they could melt down a metal object and recast it.

Some partisans might find it more efficacious to symbolize what they're giving up with tokens that are more specific to their lives. Intravenous drug users, for example, could go to an isolated spot like I mentioned above and bury the *outfit*–needle, spoon, lighter (for heroin addicts), tie, and whatever they kept it all wrapped in. When fashioning ceremonies, partisans should think carefully about what tokens and signs really epitomize the role or behaviors they're trying to get rid of.

Of all the life changes in which wandering (that aimless drifting phase of a transition) plays a key role, nowhere is it more obvious than in the transformation of the second coniunctio. At this time partisans can use planning one or even several extended periods of quiet, non-goal-oriented introspection. They could rent a cabin in the woods or desert for several days (or borrow the home of a friend who's out of town), during which time their sole purpose is to simply get to know themselves better. Write in a journal. Take long walks. Meditate. Listen to music or to nature. Let go of the need to accomplish anything except the mission that they're on. This would be a perfect time for thought discipline that I outlined in stage one. It's easy for partisans to make excuses for not allowing themselves quiet time, but the truth is that by giving this time to themselves, they stand a much better chance of being present and effective at work and at play, as well as in their roles as parent, spouse, child, sibling, and friend. This is also an opportune time to tally how effective their efforts at thought discipline have been.

The second coniunctio would also be a great time to plant and nurture a vegetable, herb, or flower garden, even if that garden is no bigger than a window box. The emergence of new life (the partisan's and the garden's) is represented in the planting of seeds, the nurturing of young plants, and then the final maturing and harvest. Preparing a special meal from this garden can evoke a strong sense of feeding yourself symbolically and literally by way of your own accomplishments thus far.

≈ V ≈

STAGE FIVE
PROJECT CHANGE

The rubedo is the third coniunctio and its color is red. Red was thought by alchemists to contain the essence of life. Medieval people believed that the soul resided in the blood, and the heart was therefore the spiritual and physical center of a person's life. From here on, the emphasis on change increases considerably, so all the baggage that partisans are carrying around from the past needs to be changed or disposed of.

Put in writing situations or events where your pride was glaring, and what this brought into your life that you like and dislike. Also write down the problems it has caused you.
The wounded male ego is the result of an attack on his pride. Most male addicts believe, or like to think of themselves as capable of taking care of themselves when it comes to physical violence. I was no exception, but I had reservations, especially by the time I was in my forties. While tending bar, I gave one of my patrons twenty dollars to get me a quarter gram of meth. He didn't. He just kept the money. My pride was hurt, so after asking him about it for a day or two, I finally walked up to him, and with both hands pushed him back a couple feet. At first I considered hitting him in the face, but my reservation kicked in, saying to me, *John, he's quite a bit bigger than you and considerably younger. You better think twice about this*." I did, which is why it was a push rather than a hit. I never got my money back, but I protected my wounded pride somewhat by doing what I did.

Write down activities you especially enjoy (except for drug and alcohol consumption).
This can be a challenge if, like me, partisans have been drinking and using since they were very young. If they can rekindle a previous interest, that's just one more thing they can occupy their time with and keep their minds off chemical substances. For many men, sports is going to be an option, and perhaps many women can take up some of the things their mother's taught them, that is if they were lucky enough to have that type of a mom.

My dad was 45 years old when I was born, so we didn't do much together like fishing, playing ball, camping, etc. Besides, he worked all night and slept days, so we didn't spend much time together during my teen and early adult years. I was only 23 when he died.

Write down a few healthy eating *and* exercise habits that you could start, and some unhealthy eating habits that you could give up.
This one can be a challenge to anyone, but very worthwhile. A majority of practicing addicts are malnourished. To help partisans recover, it's necessary to understand the impact of nutrition. It's astounding to consider that only fat contains more calories per gram than alcohol; therefore, while drinking, consumers of alcohol experience a sense of being full after having eaten very little or nothing. These *empty calories* lead to poor eating habits and malnutrition. Drug abusers experience a similar affect. Alcohol and various drugs actually keep the body from properly absorbing and breaking down nutrients and expelling toxins, which leads to a host of health problems.

Like most addicts, I was a trash can when it came to drugs, alcohol, and junk food. Practicing addicts simply don't have the time to eat right and exercise. They have more pressing drug-related things to do. Drugs and/or alcohol come first, even before family. Unfortunately, most addicts aren't capable of admitting this very disturbing fact.

Note some secret 'good' deeds that you have done or that you would like to do.
Taking stock of personal attributes doesn't mean that partisans should focus on negative ones only. Partisans should be careful with this one, because often they're charitable with selfish motives. During my addiction, I often let friends live in my home with me rent free. I thought I was being charitable, but after I got clean and thought about it, having friends living in my house was as much for me as it was for them, if not more. However, I've also done good deeds without selfish motives. I lent a hundred dollars to a friend for her mother's funeral. She didn't pay me back and I never asked for it. Also, when I left Las Vegas, I rented out my house, sold and gave away all the furniture, and sold my window cleaning business to a friend's ex wife, who I also considered my friend at the time. All I asked for the business was two hundred dollars. She didn't pay me and I never asked for it.

Put on paper occasions when you have been greedy, excessively needy, or materialistic. Keep in mind that these traits don't have to deal with drugs directly. They can be emotional, psychological, or spiritual greediness, neediness, or materialistic.
Greed is one of the cornerstones of addiction. I was at the Colorado River with friends, and I had an eight-ounce bottle of Tussionex (our drug of choice at the time). I don't know why I did it, but I consumed all of it myself when I knew very well my friends wanted some. From that time on, Susy had no use for me. That incident destroyed that relationship. However, she and my friend Terry

got some poetic justice out of the incident, because I'd gotten sick from overdosing and was throwing up for most of the day, and unable to enjoy the river.

During the latter part of my addiction, when my drug of choice was meth and I wasn't working, I'd carry a satchel around with me with items for personal hygiene, an audio cassette player, drug paraphernalia, change of underclothes, and other articles. To be able to stay high, I'd go from friend's house to friend's house, supposedly just to visit. I never asked any of them to get me high, but I'd hang around until they offered me some. I'd stay and get high with them until I noticed something in their behavior that indicated they'd probably like me to leave. Then I'd go to the next friend's house. Sometimes I wouldn't return home to my mom's house for a couple weeks. I'd say I was indeed being excessively needy. I felt justified doing that because I was unemployed.

During the entire 30 years of my addiction, I never had the money to be materialistic. I certainly would have if my financial status allowed it. Not all addicts are as indigent as I was. Many of them are even wealthy, so the materialistic part of this assignment would probably be more attributable to them.

Write down situations where you have given in to lust without regard for others, and note the problems that it caused you.
Most addicts could write a book on this one. I believe the following story speaks to this assignment adequately:

Zip, a tweaker, was attracted to Slam's wife, and when Slam was out of the room, Zip took the opportunity to look down her blouse. Slam's wife said, "Do you see something you like?"

Surprised by her boldness, Zip admitted that he did.

She said, "Well, is it worth $500?"

After thinking about it for about a millisecond, Zip said yes. She told him to be at her house around two p.m. Friday.

Zip showed up on time, paid the $500, did the wild thing with Slam's wife, then hurried away.

As usual, Slam came home from work at six p.m. and upon entering the house he asked his wife: "Hey honey, did Zip come by the house this afternoon?"

With a lump in her throat, she answered, "Uh . . . yes, he did."

Her heart skipped a beat when he asked: "And did he give you $500?"

After mustering up her best poker face, she replied: "Yeah, it's in the cookie jar, honey."

Slam, with a satisfied look on his face, said, "Good, Zip came by my work site this morning and borrowed $500. He promised to stop by here on his way home and leave the money with you."

Write down when your inner trickster has been dishonest, the problems it caused you, and whether you are ready to allow a force of some kind to

help keep you honest and direct your trickster proclivities in a more productive direction.

Most addicts could write another book on this one too. Just writing about times of shoplifting or other petty thievery isn't enough. This assignment requires some deep thinking and a lot of time. There was a period of about 15 years that I personified the trickster figure for a living. I was a salesman in service stations back before they turned into markets. We salesmen, when working on commission only, were referred to as fifty percenters, because we made fifty percent of the profit from what we sold. A hundred dollars a day was an average day. That was good money in the 70s. We carried an Elmer's Glue bottle and squirted shocks, fuel pumps, and fan clutches with hydraulic oil taken out of old shocks, telling the customer that those items were damaged and needed to be replaced. We also carried a small screwdriver that fit into our shirt pocket, along with a tire gauge and a pen. That little screwdriver was sharpened to a point to make tires leak. Another tool we carried was a short stubby screwdriver, sharpened for cutting the tires, either on the sidewall or between the tread.

Since I've gotten clean and sober, I've suffered the guilt from those years without any way to pay back all the money I stole from customers. Today, whenever I think that I've been taken advantage of by mechanics, I just pay the money and chalk it up to *what comes around goes around*.

Put in writing situations when you have been envious and jealous of others, and the problems it caused.

Definition of envy: A feeling of discontent and resentment aroused by and in conjunction with a desire for the possessions or qualities of another. Definition of jealousy: apprehensive of being displaced by a rival in affection or favor. This assignment is twofold, one for envy and one for jealousy.

One of my friends had a beautiful wife and two great kids, a new home, a moneymaking trade, a beautiful Harly Davidson sportster, and a Corvette. I lived in the projects, my wife wasn't as beautiful, but I did have a great kid. I didn't make the money that he did, and my vehicles were old and dilapidated. I was envious. This envy didn't cause problems, but there's irony here. Thirty five years later, he no longer had the beautiful wife, was still an active drug addict, no nice vehicles, medical problems that eventually took his life, a distant relationship with his kids, and not much money coming in. I don't know that he envied me, but I believe that if I were him, I would have, because I'd been clean and sober for 20 years and had earned a doctorate, published a book, was in good health, and had a wonderful relationship with my daughter. What if I hadn't gotten clean and sober? I guess I'll never know, but I'm sure I wouldn't have anything that would've made him or anyone else envious.

The most common form of jealousy as a practicing addict is aroused by spouses and lovers, but it isn't always that way. It can also occur even when we've been clean and sober for a while. One of my instructors when I was working on my doctorate was a stunningly beautiful woman. I'd say or do little things for her attention, but she saw through it. However, one of my classmates was doing the same thing, but she gave him the attention that I wanted. It finally occurred to me that I was jealous, so I gave up and thought to myself *silly me*. I offer this example from my life after recovery, but for partisans the assignment should be addressed to the years of drug and alcohol use.

Write down situations where you have avoided being responsible for your actions or lack of actions, and the problems it has caused you. Include whether you are ready to allow yourself , or some type of force to help you take responsibility for your actions?

Before I went to prison, one of my friends called me on the phone to explain--or whine (most drug addicts are whiners) about being arrested for a burglary he didn't commit. He said, "Johnny, can you believe it? The motherfuckers busted me for a burglary that I didn't do."

"Bummer man. You should be able to beat it though," I sympathized.

"Fuck, Johnny, I shouldn't have to beat the damn thing, I didn't do it. They shouldn't have arrested me in the first place."

He carried on for five minutes about the injustice of being wrongly accused. Finally, when he stopped talking long enough, I asked "Why are you so outraged about this?"

"Johnny, I didn't do it! God damn them! The bastards are trying to frame me."

"Hey Jack."

"What?"

I then calmly asked, "What about all those burglaries you didn't get caught for over the last twenty years?"

"What? Don't get carried away, Johnny! The fact is, I didn't fucking do it. This charge doesn't have anything to do with what I did before." He dismissed my question as being utterly absurd.

Nor was I one to be accountable for my actions. When I was a bartender, I was partying on band night where I worked. After sweet Sherie and I were finished dancing, I went to the bar to order another drink. Two men approached me who had been coming in the bar for the last couple of weeks. We were even on a first-name basis. They asked if I'd get them a quarter of meth. I said that I couldn't. They approached me again later, and again I was unable to. When they approached me the third time, I said yes, because a couple fellow bartenders were selling quarter grams. I got a quarter for them and took them to the back porch of the bar to make the exchange. The next day I was in the bar having a beer, and guess who walked up and flashed their badges on me?

I had experience with public defenders, so I retained another one. She was a young, fair-skinned black woman, very tall, fresh out of law school and out to save the world. She carried herself graciously, giving me the impression of an Indian goddess. The energy she put into my case really impressed me. She said I was clearly a victim of entrapment and politics. In my jury trial, she fought the case on the basis of entrapment. She fought her heart out, but her inexperience against a practiced deputy district attorney brought me a conviction.

I thought to myself: *Just my fucking luck--a clear case of entrapment and politics, and I was still convicted. The entire criminal justice system has been fucking with me for as long as I can remember. Why don't they go after child molesters and rapists? Why do they have to fuck with a fun-loving free spirit like me?*

This attitude is typical of drug addicts. One would be lucky to find one addict out of a hundred who has an internal locus of control. Almost always, they place blame outwards rather than being accountable.

I filed an appeal, of course, but that process takes a long time. As for the political implications, my public defender said that it was an election year, and that the county sheriff's department was doing a sweep in bars known for drug trafficking. This sweep was part of the incumbent sheriff's reelection campaign for his war on drugs. At the same time, the county needed to use up the fiscal year's funding provided by the state to hire extra duty vice officers so the following year's funding wouldn't be cut or diminished. Unfortunately, my attorney couldn't use any of these reasons as a defense. The truth is, if I hadn't sold drugs to undercover agents, I wouldn't have gone to prison for selling drugs. However, like my friend, Jack, I wasn't capable of seeing it that way.

Put on paper what about yourself you'd like to change most, and what you plan to do when these changes begin to manifest. Note each trait individually along with the proposed preventive behavior and how you will make change a major project in your recovery.

Everyone has things about themselves they'd *like* to change. Partisans, however, have things about themselves that they *must* change. In early recovery, one of the most glaring traits that I wanted to be rid of, was my impatience. Remember my story about when I was in the grocery store with my daughter? Because of my impatience, I threw the items I had in my arms up in the air and stormed out of the store. During early recovery, I worked on that continually. Unfortunately, it's not completely gone, and it probably never will be, but I've improved considerably. Partisans, like anyone else, are unable to completely eliminate all their flaws, but they can eliminate some of them and make others manageable.

Timing is an essential factor in inner alchemy. Often we will hear something clearly only when the time is right. Friends, colleagues, or family members may continually point out something with no results. Then later, a partisan admits that he or she has discovered a great truth that is exactly what the friend or whoever had been trying to get across all along. Timing is a great mystery, for it cannot be controlled by us. At a certain moment, an experience that would've been impossible a week before unfolds with no difficulty. The alchemists warned that all haste was of the devil; being in a hurry violates the gradual evolution that accords with time. As the Chinese philosophers well knew, to be in accord with time makes the difference between success and failure. It's not conducive to a partisan's recovery to beat themselves up when this happens, but it is conducive to their recovery to listen to what's being said by those trying to be of help like counselors, self-help groups, teachers, or spiritual advisors, which is why it is better to listen to the message rather than the messenger.

Put on paper what you've heard from friends, cohorts, family members or groups that you've actually chosen to ignore because you didn't like who was speaking.

Dennis Quaid, in *The Night the Lights Went Out in Georgia*, said something like this to a woman on a bus: "You know, I asked God why he allows me to have such bad luck, and then I heard a little voice."

"What did it say?" Asked the woman.

"It said: 'Hell, I don't know, Travis. There's just something about you that chaps my ass.'"

It's inevitable, there's going to be people that chap a partisan's ass, but sometimes those very people have a message that's eye-opening and profoundly instructive and useful, so like the old saying goes, "Don't bite the hand that feeds you."

Write down the traits that'll be most difficult to give up, and place them in what order you plan to give them up.

This is necessary because without a plan, it's too easy to let things slide. Obviously, partisans aren't going to be able to work diligently on all of them at the same time, so prioritize and keep the list close by to review periodically.

Put in writing the types of situations, stressors or pressures that cause you to regress back into your negative traits, and what you can do to lessen the likelihood of those stressors occurring.

For me, three relapses are proof enough that hanging out with old drinking and using buddies causes a regression back into the chaos of the prima materia. How can a transformation take place with such backsliding? It can't. Partisans will get trapped in a vicious cycle of what I call the revolving door of recidivism. If I hadn't come back to meetings as a newcomer after my third relapse, I doubt that my chances of a lasting and intrinsic recovery would've been possible.

In early recovery I understood the rationale behind the suggestion of not getting romantically involved for at least a year. Fresh out of prison during my first semester at the local community college, I started studying with a very attractive classmate. Eventually she was picking me up for school every morning, and it wasn't long before we ended up in bed together. I rationalized that since she was married, there wasn't a danger of the relationship developing into a long-term love affair, and eventually a relapse caused by a broken heart. I was wrong. Though the affair only lasted through the following six-week summer semester, I still developed feelings I didn't intend on developing. She broke it off because of the guilt she felt for cheating on her husband. I understood, but that didn't console my mildly broken heart. So, again I had to learn for myself the hard way what I already knew, and that's not uncommon for recovering addicts. We seem to have to learn everything the hard way, but it doesn't have to be that way. Following direction can eliminate a lot of problems if we'll just do what's suggested.

Write down what makes you lose hope and whether you can avoid those situations, and include, what people, situations, events, or thoughts restore your hope.
The fallacy of the disease concept of addiction keeps many addicts trapped in the cycle of relapse, but whether relapse is triggered by, *what's the use of trying if it's a disease?* or whether it's triggered by the lack of psychological adaptation, something causes those who relapse to lose hope first. Sometimes it's the dynamics involved with the opposite sex. If partisans are single when they start recovery, then they should wait until they've developed some stability before complicating their lives with romantic relationships. If they're in a relationship and are considering getting out of it, again they should wait before a separation or divorce–that is if it's at all possible.

Be specific when you write about how you think your life will be different without your negative traits.
As I mentioned before, one of my most glaring negative trait was impatience. I was in a hurry even when I wasn't in a hurry. During those years, I often had car accidents–sometimes involving others, but most of the time not. Being in a hurry all the time causes accidents, and because I've gotten a much better grip on my impatience problem, I don't have car accidents anymore.

During my addiction, I had an external locus of control. In other words, my finger was always pointing out in blame. Once partisans learn to stop pointing the finger, they start developing an internal locus of control. It isn't hard to imagine how much easier life can be if partisans are accountable for what happens to them. If the blame for problems remain outside of partisans, how can they possibly change it?

Write down what you are grateful for.
I've heard it said that grateful people are happy people. I believe that. It's no secret that when one is grateful for material things, they take better care of them. The same can be said of matters of the mind and soul. If partisans are truly grateful for their recovery, they'll try to protect it because it's a roadmap to a happy life. Once they get clean and sober, however, everything doesn't magically get better all of a sudden. It takes time. Partisans will still have problems, like most people do, but the kinds of problems they have are different. Most people who are grateful for their recovery are also happy.

Jot down when you were the happiest and why.
I was a happy kid, a happy-go-lucky teenager, and later a relatively happy addict. So why did I quit? Because my life was going nowhere, my family was

concerned about me, and I knew my mind and body wouldn't take the abuse much longer.

Would I change anything if I had it to do over again?

For the most part, no!

Why not?

Because I wouldn't be who I am today if my life had been lived differently. In my opinion, happiness is part of a temperament that is innate. Of course, life circumstances can alter that, but I believe that the basic temperament is static. If trauma doesn't strike, and we've had a stable and loving foundation in early childhood, most of us are capable of handling most of life's encumbrances. That's my opinion, anyway. However, I don't believe I could have remained very happy if I had not stopped drinking and using. Trauma--physical, mental, or spiritual, would have inevitably struck. I realize that there are many partisans who won't be as lucky as I was during my younger years, but that's no reason to give up. Some partisans simply have to work harder than others to achieve an internal locus of control and a happiness conducive to a successful recovery.

Put in writing your typical day's activities in terms of how much time you spend on each type of activity. Write down what you would do in a typical day if you knew that you had only one year to live.

By doing this, it's surprising what partisans can learn about themselves. *Damn, I spend a lot of time watching* TV is something I imagine a lot of addicts think. I have eliminated TV from my life completely. I have no cable, antenna, dish, or any of that. I have a couple TV sets in my home, but I don't watch television. I have a set in my gym and I watch either entertainment or educational videos when I'm on my treadmill. I have a set in my living room, but I only watch movies in the evenings, often with a friend.

Andrew Weil, a noted health guru, advises against watching the news or reading newspapers every day. He says the nonstop bad news has a negative impact on our health! Dr. Weil is right, and the reason bad news affects our health is that we know we can't do anything about it. That causes stress, a breakdown of healthy cells, and a disruption of the body's natural rhythms. I'm not saying that all partisans should do like me and eliminate television completely, but eliminating news a little at a time is a good place to start.

Write down how much time you would like to spend with loved ones.

As with all of these assignments, Partisans should spend a considerable amount of time on this one.

Put on paper what you can do to contribute to the *anima mundi* (soul of the world)—making it a better place to live.

I believe that my recovery has contributed, probably in a very small way, to the *anima mundi*. Get creative with this assignment, and don't be afraid to make your goals too lofty. Lofty is good when it comes to making the world a better place to live.

≈ VI ≈

STAGE SIX

ANGER AND RESENTMENT

Stages six and seven are imperative for an enduring peace of mind, and essential in preparing for the third coniunctio. It's very unlikely that anyone can live a happy and productive life if they're living with anger and resentment. The third coniunctio is the final destination, but partisans have the rest of their lives to maintain it. The third coniunctio is the philosopher's stone, individuation of the recovery process, the hypothetical Gold at the end of the rainbow. Like the Bakhimba in Mayombe, the third coniunctio can take from two to five years, with a rite of passage more enduring than that of the second coniunctio.

Resentment is defined as anger and ill-will caused by a real or imagined wrong or injury. Resentment is akin to having a pet rattlesnake. Half the time it just lays there, kind of lazy and quiet and inconspicuous. When something stirs it up like a noise, a movement, or a threat, the snake coils, hisses, and then strikes. The fangs sink in and poison is injected into the victim's bloodstream, sometimes ending in death. The main difference is that when partisans get resentful, they also strike at themselves, and the poison that runs through their veins is of their own making.

Unreasonable resentment is a hallmark of addiction, and recovery is compromised unless partisans learn to let go of resentments, anger, and hatred. Abandoning resentments is one of the most crucial things partisans can do for themselves and the people they love. I realize that for some people this sounds corny and possibly unrealistic.

Notice that resentment is caused by real or *imagined* injury. That's a considerable point to remember, because chemically dependent people are experts at conjuring up wrongs that they imagine have been committed against them. This susceptibility to injury cramps their lives and causes them to become guarded, suspicious, and jealous.

Resentment always has at its base certain negative, irrational thoughts. Partisans need to figure out which irrational thoughts are making them angry and work on shooing them away.

They need to ask themselves if they're carrying around unreasonable resentments? They would do well to scrutinize any resentment they think is reasonable. Do they run negative, blaming statements through their minds until they're so upset they can hardly sleep? If they're truly honest, they probably have at least one resentment that's causing them anguish. Partisans need to write down their resentments–the names of whom they resent, then why they are resentful.

This is an important exercise because, while it's easy for partisans to sit back and say, "Yeah, what's his name really had an attitude." It's extremely difficult for partisans to see their own unreasonable beliefs, thoughts, and attitudes. They usually can't rid themselves of their resentments until they recognize them. It's a good idea for them to save their resentment list, because they'll need to come back to it.

Anger and resentments are caused, maintained, and intensified by thinking patterns. Addicts characteristically dwell on injustices and resentments, letting them smolder for hours, days, weeks, months, even years after what provoked it has passed. My mom, for example, used to gripe at my dad for things that occurred twenty years before. Partisans may think they live in the present, but their emotions are usually stuck in their puerile past. They often don't recognize their own thinking patterns.

The key to getting control of resentment, is to learn to think differently. Like I did on the prison yard, partisans can shoo away the old thoughts and replace them with new ones.

This is essential for partisans to understand. If they can't accept the simple fact that their thinking controls their feelings, they'll never be able to change, or be able to find the key to a happy life. Their lives will continue to be filled with hassles, anxiety, and resentments.

Those who suffer from chemical dependency have another problem that doesn't always look like it's related to anger, but it is, and that's self-pity, which is caused by thinking negative thoughts.

Addicts typically feel so sorry for themselves because people like family members, friends, co-workers, lovers, and the rest of the world doesn't give them what they deserve. As they're swimming around in the pity pot, they seldom stop to consider whether what they're asking of others is reasonable. Like many other addicts, they make unreasonable demands and are devastated when they aren't met. To complicate things, some of the demands of addicts are never spoken. They just expect other people to know what they want. How unreasonable is that? Self-pity is a form of anger. They're angry that life isn't fair, that it's full of hardship and disappointment. They think of themselves as victims tossed around by an uncaring society. They're often strong believers in luck, too. Bad luck for them, and good luck for everyone else. They're usually chronic blamers as well, blaming anyone who's around: spouses, kids, society, government, and especially members of law enforcement. I'm not saying that all addicts have all of this issues, but these issues are common among addicts.

The most common targets of an addict's blame are the very people they're dependent on. A typical addict might say, "It was my husband's (or wife's, or parents, or child's) fault.

Most addicts are experts at the blame game. If they can't find a person to blame, they'll even blame God. Self-pity, resentment, and fault-finding are symptoms of disorder in many families. Part of the recovery process is fearlessly confronting these defects in thinking.

Partisans should consider the things that make them angry. Their unruly kids, asshole colleagues, self-centered spouses, undependable cars and computers, snippy waitresses, employers who don't appreciate their worth, nosy relatives, and the list goes on. Addicts commonly think that people are always trying to bullshit, manipulate, and trick them. That's because they're usually trying to bullshit, manipulate, and trick others. They also get insulted, ridiculed, and used. Life treats them unfairly. Considering all that, they think it's their right to be resentful.

Everybody has problems. The problems that addicts have are no more disturbing than anyone else's. Those who look like they're sitting on top of the world usually have just as many problems and tragedies as addicts do. They just seem to handle them better.

Partisans shouldn't think of themselves as special, but they can get that way. They can become special by learning to cope with their problems and resentments without destroying their self-worth or trampling all over someone else's feelings. They cope with their problems by learning to be accountable for their own happiness.

Many of those in recovery believe that their lives have been nothing but one bad break after another. Their blood boils at the mere thought of the hassles that family, bosses, and so-called buddies have put them through. Those people *make them* resentful and unhappy.

This simply isn't true. Addicts can make themselves resentful by illogical thinking. They blame other people for their troubles. Like my dad used to say: "Don't make a mountain out of a mole hill." Partisans can turn everyday irritations into major calamities. They get resentful because they're thinking of all the things that just aren't fair.

Partisans should stop and think. They need to analyze their thinking, and listen to what they're saying to themselves. Many of them have these kinds of thoughts and they get resentful because of them. Their feelings of resentment are triggered by their negative, irrational, catastrophic thoughts. And here's something that shouldn't be ignored. Partisans can't afford to get into a frazzle over minor annoyances. They shouldn't waste their energy turning molehills into mountains. They don't have time to spin their wheels about trivialities and turn them into crises.

Partisans will *seem* to never have enough time, because they have real catastrophes to deal with, like medical problems such as hep c, unruly children, making up to people they've hurt with their arrogant and selfish behavior, rebuilding a career left in the rubble of addiction, and rebuilding their lives.

There's work to be done. If partisans are to fully recover, they must learn to put the petty irritations of everyday life into their proper perspectives. They should take responsibility for their behavior and stop blaming others for their mistakes. I'm repeating myself intentionally because I know there'll be partisans reading this. It's typical in early recovery, and I say this from experience. We know we're screwed up and it's not easy being continually reminded of it, so it's easy to read stuff like this and then blow it off because "it really doesn't apply to me." Or, reading the words and thinking about something else. Who hasn't done that?

It's hard for partisans to say things like, what's the big deal if Jim was a day late coming home from his fishing trip? What's the big deal if someone stole a parking spot? For these types of things, partisans can get ready to start a major war, and then develop a resentment. They can risk their recovery by stubbornly clinging to resentments. Life is too short, and recovery is too precious, to squander serenity on petty bullshit.

Partisans can learn how to cope with their unreasonable resentments. First, they must forcefully analyze away the illogical and self-defeating commentary that's running through their heads. Second, should practice and keep practicing the thought discipline I've outlined in stage one.

Put in writing all the people that you have mistreated by your addiction, and the effect on them and on you and on your relationship with them.
In stage three partisans were asked to write down what broken relationships with the opposite sex or friends they've had, and explain how those broken relationships hurt them. There's been more people in the partisans' lives over the years than members of the opposite sex and friends, which is the reason for this very similar assignment.

In stage five partisans were asked to write down when their inner trickster had been dishonest and the problems it caused. Both of those assignments are similar, but not the same. More often than not, partisans are going to have to dig deep into the damaged memory and retrieve more ways that they have mistreated people. They don't have to be people they know, but they can be, if they haven't already discussed them in previous assignments.

I explained how I used to rip off travelers as a fifty percenter in service stations, but I didn't mention how I ripped off the people I worked for. During the time I was a salesman in the station business, I noticed how terribly upset the owners got when they suspected a salesman of stealing from them. They hired people to steal *for* them, and then couldn't understand why they would steal *from* them. While I wasn't stealing much from them compared to what I made stealing for them, I still stole quite a bit of money from them over time. I didn't see a problem with that. I do now because they paid me to do a job and I should've stuck to that. There were a couple station owners I worked for whom I sincerely liked, and I did feel guilty for stealing from them. However, one would think that I'd have some guilt from what I was doing to their customers, but I didn't. Of course, I do now.

Write down what you could do to make up for what you've done to each of the people you mistreated or abused in some way, and the consequences you fear in accomplishing this. Include the worst and the best things that can happen, and what you think will happen next time.

I wrote a letter to my second wife in an attempt to make up for my behavior after she left me. I didn't have her address so the letter rested on my computer for many years. In 2010 I got her phone number from her sister and called her. I no longer had the letter on my computer, but I told her about it. She accepted it, but I don't believe she was honest in her response, in that she was too understanding, accepting, and agreeable. My guess was that she didn't want to admit to me what she really went through. All of that was none of my business anyway. I did what I called her to do. My experience taught me that it doesn't matter whether those I've mistreated accept my efforts or not.

Write down whether you feel angry or resentful toward any people that you have mistreated. Examine and record the thoughts that make you angry and resentful.
This isn't asking for the same thing twice. The first sentence refers to *feelings* toward others, whereas the second sentence is in regard to *thinking* prior to feelings. This is one of those assignments where one should evaluate how much time and thought went into it. It requires the partisan to think. Often partisans, usually men (and I was one of them), have a difficult time separating feeling from thinking.

Put in writing any other ways or methods you've used, or are going to use, to get rid of anger and resentment toward those you have mistreated.
If I were given this assignment after my second wife left me, I would probably have been at a loss to come up with anything. If something similar happened to me now, however, I would use thought discipline to change the angry thoughts. By doing that I would be getting rid of the angry thoughts and replacing them with ones that didn't make me *feel* angry.

STAGE SEVEN

RECTIFICATION

Of course, partisans shouldn't try reconciliation if it will cause more problems. Nor should they use this as an excuse not to make the attempt. After everyone who's been mistreated is documented, along with the essential homework in connection with it from stage six, then the partisan is ready to start a process that sometimes takes years. This is one of those stages that doesn't always get finished, but it's necessary to stay conscious of it and apply it whenever the opportunity arises.

In seeking to mend a fractured relationship, a well-considered strategy is as crucial to success as showing sincerity and humility. Partisans need to empathize, apologize, repair, and take the necessary steps to ensure they don't repeat their mistakes.

It's also helpful for partisans to measure how debilitating their wrongdoings were. A critical evaluation of their mistakes is necessary for developing empathy. They need to look at their actions from different perspectives, mostly from the perspectives of those they wronged. The reason for this is to determine how and why their behavior hurt other people. Makes sense.

Partisans should realize how serious rectification is. Everyone's been wronged, and one of the worst aspects of a rectification is when anger isn't given the seriousness it should. Therefore, empathy with the mistreated person is essential.

When partisans approach those they've mistreated, they should suggest specific ways to rectify the harm done. Suggestions should fit the wrong done, if possible. This can be thought of as damage control and the efforts required to clean up a mess.

If partisans let lovers down, they should look for ways to strengthen the relationships and show devotion to them and their needs. If confidence has been broken and something was said that shouldn't have been said, then partisans need to rebuild the relationship over time through actions and activities that indirectly restore that person's faith and trust in them.

Partisans should be careful not to make suggestions that seem like an effort to buy their way out, such as: "Let me take you to dinner." Also, avoid asking those who were harmed questions like, "How can I make this up to you?" or "What can I do to fix this?" Partisans need to come up with a way to make it right themselves. It's their responsibility.

It'll be helpful for partisans to look back on this experience: It's often unpleasant, and they'll probably need to do it again later. It's usually unavoidable, but preferably not for the same mistake, so partisans will need to reexamine how their mistakes were made and how they can avoid them in the future.

Write down what you've done so far to make up for how you've harmed others. These can include apologies, helpful tasks for those that you've mistreated, changed attitudes, etc. This work is usually *more* than just apologies, but sometimes an apology is all that's possible.

Some partisans will be hard-pressed finding people they've done harm too. Other than my mistreatment of ex-wives and the man's house I burglarized, when I got clean and sober, I didn't have anyone to contact. Most of the harm I did to people were those from so many years before that I couldn't find them. This is common with addicts, like me, who was using drugs and alcohol for so many years. I was in my twenties and early thirties when I was stealing from employers. I was 45 when I got clean, so contacting them came to a dead end. Again, be honest and don't use this as an excuse not to make the attempt.

Write down if there are apologies that you need to make that doesn't require reconciliation and then explain why. Explaining why is important because an apology might not be enough.

Here's a story about redemption, which is what rectification is all about, and specific to this assignment. I'll call the main character Scumbag. When Scumbag walked into his apartment, his answering machine light was blinking. It was one of his ex-girlfriends.

"Scumbag, this is Jackie, please give me a call. I really need to talk to you."

He dialed the number and sat down on his chair next to the telephone.

"Hello."

"How ya doing, old girlfriend? Is your killer body still turning heads like it always has?"

"You're sweet, Scumbag, I don't care what everybody says about ya. Hey, my mom is really struggling right now, and I was wondering if you could do me a big favor."

"If I can. What is it?"

"My mom's car broke down. She called her mechanic to come and tell her what it would cost to fix, but she can't afford the parts. She needs a carburetor. If she doesn't get the car running, she can't go to work and she'll lose her job."

"Jackie, you're in luck. If you'll bring over a pint of tequila, I'll furnish the pot. I have the very carburetor that fits your mom's car."

"Scumbag, are you propositioning me?"

"No, I just miss hangin' out with ya. Come on over and get the carburetor. Your mom needs it, so you can have it."

Jackie came over and knocked on the door. "Thanks, for the carburetor, Scumbag, and for saving my Mom's job. I really appreciate it."

"I didn't steal that carburetor for your mom, you know. On my way out of a wrecking yard, it was just sitting there asking to be taken, and there wasn't anyone around."

"You stole it! My God, Scumbag, my mom can't be putting stolen merchandise on her car."

"Would I put your mom in a position to go to jail? C'mon, take the carburetor, it's used, and I guarantee there's no way to trace it."

"Are you sure?" Jackie asked with a distrustful look in her eye.

"I promise. If anything like that happens, I will let you hit me as hard as you can in the head with a hammer."

"Okay, but I doubt if I would take the chance if she didn't really need it badly."

"Do you remember that rowdy-looking biker dude, Hercules, that I used to boost with?"

"No, not really."

"Well, he was six feet four, 250 pounds, with tattoos all over his body, and he was the bully type. He used his size to get what he wanted. Anyway, one day me and him were out boosting car parts in garages and gas stations and we went into this little garage in San Bernardino."

"Is this going to be a long one, Scumbag?"

"No, it's a short one, and I have a good reason for telling it."

"Okay, but I can't stay much longer."

"Yeah, yeah. Anyway, when this mechanic wouldn't buy anything, Hercules didn't like it. Jackie, this little mechanic had a gimpy leg and big thick glasses. I couldn't believe it. Hercules started to push this poor little guy around, so I said, 'c'mon Herc, let em alone. He doesn't want to buy. Let's go.' Then Hercules said to me: 'Shut up you little scumbag, I'll take care of this.'"

"That bastard!"

"Jackie, I couldn't believe he said that to me, so I picked up a pipe wrench and hit 'em up side of the head with it. Anyway, I didn't connect very well, so now I've got this fuckin' monster coming after me. He hit me and I went sailing across the garage, landing on an old car seat that was sitting on the floor. Well, in schools of martial arts, they tell us not to use our talent unless we have to, because our bodies are considered deadly weapons, and we can go to jail."

"You don't know martial arts, Scumbag!" Jackie retorted and laughing at the same time.

"How do you know what I know?"

"Never mind, go on with your story," Jackie said rolling her eyes back.

Well shit, I was committing a felony anyway, so I came flying off that old car seat and caught him with my foot, but a car was in the way and it didn't knock him down. So I got him to the ground with an y-pa-soi-nagi, then chopped him in the adams-apple. As he was . . . What are you laughing at?"

"Nothing, Scumbag. Hurry up, I've gotta go."

"Anyway, as he was laying their gasping for air and squirming around, I told the mechanic to get out of there, call the police, and not come back till they got here."

"Wow, Scumbag. I'm really impressed. You actually placed that little man before your own needs. That's really gallant."

"I realize I am usually thought of as a despicable junky, but I've told you this because I really don't want you to worry about your mom getting in trouble for putting stolen property on her car. I just wouldn't put her at that kind of risk."

"Wow, Scumbag. I'm beginning to realize that you are like that Don Quixote guy in the *Man of La Mancha*."

"Yeah, I've always been one to protect the underdog."

Jackie nudges his shoulder with her forehead. "I wonder why that is."

"Probably because I'm an underdog."

Scumbag was a liar and thief, and he owed Jackie an apology. There's not much he could do to make up for the little lies he told her, but she definitely had an apology coming for lying about where he got the carburetor, because it came out of a parts-store where he worked for a short time. Also, this story reveals something good about ole Scumbag. We see his humanity (defending the mechanic) that's not always apparent when we think of addicts. Just because addicts have done bad things, don't necessarily make them bad people. If Scumbag was working in this stage of recovery, his attributes should be listed as well as his character flaws.

Rehearse reconciliations by using *imaginal dialogues.*

Before becoming familiar with Imaginal Dialogues and Jung's concept of active imagination, I spent a lot of time talking to myself (out loud, I might add) when I was alone--usually at home or driving in my car. I still do this, but I have learned to apply this in a different way and benefit from it. These conversations are between me and someone else, usually someone I know. I am usually trying to convince someone, let's say my friend Jack, to accept my point of view about something; therefore, I have two people in my head in dialogue, and both of them have a point of view.

Previously, my description of this behavior was that I was simply talking to myself. When this voice answered me, it was not my friend, the human Jack. It was my *image* of him. It was the Jack *in me* that answered. I then needed to place Jack in a didactic position, and allow him to argue his case. My real life friend Jack is very argumentative, so I had to really think in order to be able to imagine what he'd say if he was really there. This process required nurturing, and I finally mastered it. Often I have to lose an argument to Jack to learn something. I don't always use Jack's image, sometimes it's Rich, and sometimes others, depending on the issue. Apparently, the "I" has very little control over the spontaneous thoughts and images that pop up. I am often able to accept Jack's and Rich's positions, or that of others, in order to come to the best conclusion. This is a form of active imagination called imaginal dialogues.

Everybody uses imagination. It works in recognizable ways, like memory and problem solving, and in ways that are not so apparent or simply understood. A lot of imagination and its capacities and functions remain a mystery.

Imagery, as a product of imagination, uses all five senses. For example, the sound of a horn, the taste and smell of watermelon, the touch of a dog, as well as visual images. Imagery has the capacity to grab our attention and involve us in an unrestricted range of experience, from simple representations of the material world to outrageous adventures in strange, new places. So it is with rehearsing reconciliations using imaginal dialogues.

Read to a friend or associate what you've done so far toward reconciliation, and ask if it sounds sincere enough. Record their responses.
When using friends, partisans should not look for one that is likely to agree with anything asked of them. They should select one who will be honest enough to say that sincerity is lacking and why. By recording their answers, partisans can build a data base to use when attempting reconciliation with others.

After you have had your first encounter, write down (1) what happened, (2) how you felt about it, (3) how the other person responded, (4) what you learned from it, and (5) what you would do differently.
As I said before, making things right to people who've been mistreated will probably take a long time for most, but that's no reason to put it off. For best results, it should be done as soon as possible.

After having rectified harm done to others, write down your overall impressions, whether anything surprised or disappointed you, and which ones were the most difficult to accomplish.
Sometimes, partisans aren't going to get the impression that they've done any good at all. That's inevitable, and it could happen two or three times in a row. Attempts like that can put a damper on good intentions, but once a few of them are over with, there will likely be incidents that happen that are surprising and maybe even amazing. When that happens, it makes it much easier to continue with more.

Write down how you are dealing with having to defend yourself?
If partisans have made an honest effort toward rectifying harm done, they will undoubtedly have issues with some, and pleasant memories of others. Many partisans will be resentful at times, so all of these feeling-based issues should be written down. Once finished, it's also a good idea to store them in a safe place. There will come a day in the future when partisans will find it interesting to read and reflect about.

Describe in writing the conversations in your imaginal dialogues.
The best way for partisans to do this is to put themselves in the other's shoes and ask some critical questions: How did my mistakes affect their lives? Did my mistakes cause irreversible damage to people's self worth? Were they dependent on me for anything? Did I let them down?

This function of recreating material reality in the imagination is closely related to what Gestalt therapists refer to as immediacy of experience. This is different from merely thinking about or contemplating an event: It is living the event through all the senses. This quality of imagination, immediacy of experience, makes a number of benefits possible. An increased awareness of the partisan occurs on an emotional, cognitive, and physical level as a result of events experienced in imaginal dialogues. An increased awareness of self in the moment is crucial to the healing process.

≈ VIII ≈

STAGE EIGHT

DEVELOPING
AN INTERNAL LOCUS OF CONTROL

A majority of addicts have a seemingly natural tendency to *not* accept when they've been wrong. There's no shortage of ordinary people, for that matter, who'll accept when they're wrong. The philosopher's stone cannot be achieved unless partisans are capable of doing this, despite how embarrassing or humiliating it might be, or how much it deflates their egos. To address this, Partisans should develop an internal locus of control

Individuation of the recovery process is a status that not all, even many seemingly recovered addicts, actually achieve. How can partisans be elevated to the ultimate level if they still operate on an external locus of control? The philosopher's stone--*the gold*--can't be achieved unless an internal locus of control has been mastered. If partisans place blame 'out there' and not take ownership of their part in it, then they are operating in an *ex*ternal locus of control. If partisans are truly accountable for all of their actions and are unhesitatingly willing to accept when they're wrong, then they can say that they're operating on an internal locus of control. But this takes practice, and those who work on it diligently, will be better people because of it:

Put in writing a plan to allow time for reflection each day.
In early recovery, I was a student at the community college level. During my first semester, I was enrolled in a computer science course. In that course, our instructor taught us how to make a macro for our daily journal. Opening our journal, but not reading it, was how the instructor took roll. If there was no journal entry for that date, then the instructor knew that the student wasn't there. We could write anything we wanted and it wouldn't be read. With that journal, which I continued to use after the course was over, I reflected on all the issues that were going through my mind every day. I used a computer, but those who don't have access to one or don't know how to use one, can still use the old-fashioned method with pen and paper.

Write down new behaviors that you would like to try to make your journey of recovery more effective, and record how you will go about implementing them.

Partisans shouldn't spend much time alone, unless they're sleeping. The old cliche, *idle time is the devil's workshop*, applies more to those in recovery than it does to most people. The 12-step precept of HALT—not getting too *hungry, angry, lonely, or tired* should also be adhered to. It's during those times that partisans are most susceptible to relapse.

Of course, hunger describes a lack of food. Most people are aware of how necessary it is to have regular nutritional meals, the best being small in size and frequent. Hunger can also point toward emotional needs: hunger for attention, for comfort, for understanding, or for companionship. It's also necessary that partisans have others in their lives who can give them moral support, whether it's non using friends, members of various groups, or work related company. Just like we all need grocery stores to take care of physical hunger, partisans need the community of like-minded people to fill their needs for socialization. Therefore, solutions to social hunger are association with other like-minded people.

Anger is more complex and the solution can be more challenging for partisans. There's nothing wrong with feeling anger! Most addicts, however, haven't learned how to express anger constructively. The way they express anger often takes destructive form. They either turn anger against themselves or others. Anger can range from criticizing and belittling to name-calling and physical violence. Sometimes anger is part of a partisan's very being. In that case, it's usually connected to childhood trauma. Refer to stage six for anger and resentment.

Being lonely refers to isolating oneself. It is similar to hunger in that the solution is the same, namely other people. However, loneliness points to the difficulty of reaching out. This can have many causes, one being that isolation was a childhood survival tool, the other being emotional or clinical depression. If loneliness is either a constant or frequent companion, and there doesn't seem to be a way out of it, professional help may be necessary.

Everybody has a tendency to ignore tiredness at times. I once saw a video of an experiment in which volunteers were subjected to either alcohol intake or sleep deprivation. Being physically tired may be the cause of as many traffic accidents as alcohol consumption. It is a serious condition that endangers our well-being as well as that of others. The solution is of course getting plenty of sleep at night or taking naps during the day. If partisans have prolonged difficulty sleeping at night, they should see a health-care provider. The other form of tiredness comes from taking on too much, being overloaded and overwhelmed -- an almost universal condition in the busy lives of many people.

Discuss on paper the negative thinking that so many recovering addicts have such a hard time letting go of, and include what strategies you plan to use to avoid it.

Addicts often think negatively. They simply have bad attitudes. These attitudes consist of negativity, blaming, and being chronically dissatisfied. These types of thinking is a common symptom with all types of addictions. Partisans will probably suffer from it at one time or another, and it doesn't go away with a spin dry in a rehab. It clings to addicts even when they're clean and sober, all too often sabotaging their efforts at recovery.

What follows are eight well-known patterns of negative thinking that partisans should evaluate and discuss with friends, relatives, or colleagues.:

1. Assumptions
This pattern is characterized by broad, general assumptions based on one incident or piece of evidence. Assumption usually takes the form of absolute statements with words such as all, every, none, never, always, everybody and nobody. For example, if someone were to read too much personal development literature, they might believe that *all* television programming is bad. Partisans can stop thinking in absolute terms by using words such as, some, often, many, sometimes, and most. Saying that some, or even most television is bad is much easier to take seriously than saying *all* of it is.

2. Radical Thinking
This type of thinking doesn't allow room for gray areas. People and objects become either right or wrong, good or bad, smart or stupid. Partisans should resist making these types of judgements by accepting people and objects as they are, because people and objects are usually too complex to be reduced to either/or judgements. This is critical in regards to partisans judging themselves. They need to allow themselves some room to make mistakes without automatically labeling themselves as stupid, wrong, or incompetent.

3. Tunnel Vision
This is focusing on one element of a situation to the exclusion of everything else. For example, let's say a partisan is interviewed by a local radio station. Rather than focusing on the success of the interview, the partisan's after-thoughts are distracted by a few negative comments by newspaper reviewers. To break this pattern, they need to make an effort to shift their focus to the opposite frame of mind. In this case, they could focus on positive feedback rather than the negative.

4. Telepathy
This common pattern with addicts occurs when they make snap judgements about others. They might, for example, think of a job interviewer as a loser because of a facial expression. This could be based on intuition, past experiences, or projection, whereby partisans imagine that people feel the same way they do and react to things in the same manner they do. While their thinking might occasionally be true, they will often turn out to be wrong. Maybe the interviewer just then thought of something distasteful? A good way to handle

this pattern is to treat judgement-calls about people as guesses to be tested and checked. Get evidence before making judgement-calls about people.

5. Disasterizing

This occurs when a partisan's imagination focuses on the likelihood of tragedy and disaster. These thoughts often start with the words "What if?" What if I fail the exam? What if my car breaks down? What if I don't get a promotion? Such statements create anxiety and stress. One of the best ways to deal with this is to evaluate a situation in terms of probability. Are the chances of disaster one in a million? Or, are they closer to one in a hundred? Or maybe they're only one in fifty or even ten.

6. Exaggeration

This involves blowing things out of proportion. Like my dad used to say to me: "Stop making mountains out of mole hills." Helpful hints become harsh criticisms. Simple mistakes become tragic events. Minor obstacles become overwhelming hurdles. To overcome this, partisans should pay attention to the language they use. They should stop using words such as disgusting, awful and terrible. They can also eliminate phrases like "It's unbearable." Usually, it is bearable. History has shown over and over again that most people can cope with almost any psychological blow and can endure incredible physical pain.

7. Limited Thinking

This can take two forms. First, partisans will often directly compare themselves to other people. For example, "She writes far better than me." Other comparisons might actually be favorable, such as "I am prettier than her." Either way, there is an underlying assumption that one's worth is questionable. Consequently, partisans can seek out ways to test their value and measure themselves against others. Limited thinking can be broken by recognizing that most comparisons are meaningless. Everyone has strong and weak points.

8. Shoulda's. Woulda's and Coulda's

In this last pattern, partisans usually live according to a set of inflexible rules about how they and other people should behave. They have a fixed view of what is right, and those who deviate from their values or standards are bad. Addicts are just as hard on themselves. Some common and unreasonable "shoulds" include:

"I should never lose an argument"
"I should always be confident"
"I should never be wrong"
"I should always be content"

To overcome this, partisans should try to have greater flexibility in the rules and expectations they feel compelled to live by. And when it comes to other people, it is best to accept their individuality. Partisans should accept that other people won't always live according to their values.

Write down all of your triggers for relapse, and how you can guard against them or prepare for them.
High risk factors such as being around people who are drinking or using, having an unexpected argument with an employer, or going through an especially stressful day at work, make partisans vulnerable for relapse. A trigger is anything that causes sudden stress, pain, or discomfort. High risk factors in people's lives cause internal dysfunctions. With partisans these factors are triggers that need to be recognized as such. Once a trigger occurs, partisans develop symptoms of internal dysfunction. These symptoms include difficulty in thinking clearly, managing feelings and emotions, and remembering unpleasant things. Partisans will tend to overreact to stress, have difficulty sleeping restfully, and have more accidents if they don't develop an awareness of common risk factors and triggers.

Relapse triggers can affect partisans who encounter people, situations, or settings they associate with past drug use. They often experience strong urges to use drugs or alcohol. Such cue-induced relapses, can occur long after a partisan has stopped using. Certain triggers set off their desire for food, substances, and behaviors. All advertising is designed to trigger human impulses. Situations, people, weather, and times of day can all be triggers too. They can be overwhelming or subtle. When addicts stop using, they make progress toward recovering from their addiction. The danger, however, of relapse is a constant threat to the chances of full recovery. Here are some common triggers:

- *Being around drugs or alcohol, other addicts, or places where substances are sold*
- *Negative feelings, particularly anger, sadness, loneliness, guilt, fear, and anxiety*
- *Positive feelings that create a need to celebrate*
- *Boredom*
- *Over-the-counter drug use*
- *Physical pain*
- *Listening to drinking and using stories*
- *Coming into a lot of cash*
- *Using prescription drugs that cause euphoria even if used properly*
- *Becoming complacent.*

Put on paper how you can make up for or remedy something when you find out you were wrong.
Once partisans develop an internal locus of control, they're capable of recognizing wrongs from the past that they didn't recognize as such at the time. They're sometimes incapable of recognizing these wrongs in early recovery or when working in the earlier stages. They can also become capable of recognizing present justifying behavior and putting a stop to it.

STAGE NINE

"ANIMA MUNDI COLENDAE GRATIA"
(for the sake of tending soul in the world)

If partisans were contumacious assholes during their addiction, then this stage serves as a monitor to keep them in check so they won't remain that way. Everybody needs introspection, but far from everybody participates in this spiritual notion. The world can be viewed as hostile or amicable. Partisans can't achieve individuation of the recovery process--the philosopher's stone--if they don't view their fellow men and women as partners rather than antagonists. Life isn't a contest.

The world is a living spiritual entity. This was understood by the ancient philosophers and the alchemists who referred to the spiritual essence of the world as the *anima mundi*—the soul of the world. The alchemists explored the *anima mundi*. While the church during the renaissance looked for light in the heavens, the alchemists sought the light hidden in matter. They understood that there was a sacred essence in the fabric of creation, which through their experiments and imagination they worked to release. For the alchemists the *anima mundi* is the divine spark in matter, the "philosophical mercury," which is the universal and scintillating fire in the light of human nature.

Alchemy was originally concerned with turning base metal into gold, liberating the light hidden in the darkness, the fiery sparks of the world soul—that is the light of nature, dispersed or sprinkled throughout the structure of the world. The alchemists also understood that there is a connection between the *anima mundi* and the soul or innermost aspects of man. The source of the wisdom and knowledge of the all-pervading essence of the *anima mundi* was the innermost and most secret numinosum of man.

The tradition of alchemy reinterpreted into the language of inner transformation can be thought of as a key to help partisans liberate their natural light and to transform the world. The context in which I am using the *anima mundi*, is in making the world a better place to be.

A meaningful part of growth and motivation as human beings lies in contributing to the greater good, being part of something greater than us. While making the world a better place often calls to mind images of great leaders at the head of impressive social movements, white-coated researchers developing new medicines or energy sources, or geniuses dreaming up theories that explain the world around us, there is plenty of room for fewer lofty acts that create small measures of happiness in the lives of those around us. Here are nine suggestions for partisans:

1. <u>Give compliments</u>: Partisans can tell people how much they like the job they're doing, how much they like their outfit or new haircut, their singing voice--whatever. They should be honest and sincere by practicing casual compliments, like sending an out-of-the-blue email to someone whose website, blog, post, or comment they really like. The spiritual aspect of doing so doesn't require anything in return, just letting someone know that something they're doing works, is good enough

I had the lawn in front of my house removed and replaced with rock. I've received several compliments on it, so after writing the preceding paragraph, I thought it would be a good idea to practice what I preach, so I called the owner of the landscaping company and told him about the compliments and how happy I am with the job he did. Doing little things like that really does contribute to the *anima mundi*, and at the same time makes us feel better. It did me.

2. <u>Be open</u>: Partisans can let people know exactly how they feel about something that's on their minds. Nothing negative. There's a different propriety for that. Partisans often keep too much to themselves, so letting someone into their confidence can be a good way to show trust and appreciation. Of course, partisans have to judge what is and isn't appropriate. It is possible to move past openness to dragging others into partisan problems, and that's not contributing to the *anima mundi*.

3. <u>Offer someone a book or video</u>: Making a gift of something a partisan has read or viewed and enjoyed is more than just a nice gesture, it's a way of showing someone that they're being thought of and understood, and that the partisan wants to share something with them. The gesture doesn't end when they take the book or video. After they've read or viewed it, they can talk about it together .

4. <u>Make something for someone</u>: Baking a cake, writing a poem, painting a Christmas ornament, anything artistic, and giving it to someone for no apparent reason are good ideas. Like giving someone a book, it tells people that partisans think about them and wanted to do something nice. Because it's something they made, makes it more personal. Give without expectations, whether they return the favor or not, whether they like it or not, whether they're nice to you or not, these responses are all irrelevant. Like the old saying goes, it's the thought that counts.

5. <u>Send a letter, email, or text message out of the blue</u>: Partisans can email someone they haven't spoken to for a while, or text someone they see every day

just to be nice. Maybe they'll respond, maybe they won't, but that doesn't matter. At least they'll know that they're important enough to be thought of–that is, unless they're prone to being cynical.

6. <u>Give an employer a compliment about an employee</u>: It's one thing to tip or say something nice to someone for their service, it's another to contact their boss and tell them what a good job they've done. If partisans don't have time at the moment, they can get the employee's name and call, email, or write a letter. Far too often, it's the other way around. Many people won't hesitate to complain rather than compliment.

7. <u>Teach someone how to do something</u>: Partisans can share their skill or talent with someone by showing them how to do something. It contributes to their knowledge base. Partisans should have patience and respect for the person they're helping. Partisans are giving them a gift, not compensating for some lack in their character.

When I was a student tutor, I let one of my tutees come to my home where I tutored him on my computer. He was a challenge because he was slow. Every day, the first thing he'd say is, "What do I do?" It took him a week to learn how to open Microsoft Word. So, the challenge for me was managing my impatience.

8. <u>Recognize someone's assets</u>: Openly observe someone's talent by letting them take over a presentation, deferring to their wisdom, asking them advice, or otherwise *flex their talent muscles*. Especially if they're a subordinate, giving them a chance to make an impression shows that a partisan trusts and appreciates them, as well as allowing them to get the attention they deserve.

9. <u>Bring people together</u>: Partisans could introduce two friends or colleagues who they believe have something to gain from each other. Partisans will be letting both of them know that they value them, and maybe create a partnership that will make everyone concerned better off.

I realize some partisans will think a couple of these are corny, but they're just suggestions. Perhaps these suggestions will trigger other ideas. Start from number one and do each one of these, then write down what you did.

Snowballs gain momentum and get bigger when they're rolled down a hill. Put in writing a time when your life started going downhill and you were able to stop it before it got worse.
This one will be a challenge for most partisans because, like me, this practice usually hasn't entered their minds during their addiction. The only example from my life comes from early recovery during my first semester at the local community college. Back then financial aide students were required to be enrolled in four 18 week courses at the same time. About half way through that semester, things were piling up as a result of procrastination. I knew I'd either have to bear down and get papers started and study for exams right away, or get

so overwhelmed that I'd be forced to drop out. Fortunately, I was able to get it all done with a 3.5 GPA for my first semester. That was stressful. From then on, however, I started on papers and studied for exams as soon as possible. I never felt that stress again during the rest of my college career and I held that 3.5 all the way through my doctorate.

Put on paper how you would describe your overall outlook and beliefs concerning humanity.
Many partisans will be compelled to write just anything to complete the assignment. None of these assignments should be approached that way. If their outlooks and beliefs concerning humanity are negative or prophetically dismal, then that's what they should write. Hopefully, that will change with time. Some people look at a glass as half empty while others look at it as half full. The hope is, that as a clean and sober life begins to improve, that glass will start appearing half full rather than half empty.

Write down your favorite sources of wisdom and knowledge about healthy values. Here are some topics. Address each one of them on paper.
- Nutrition
- Education
- Stress management
- Sexuality
- Time management
- Goal setting
- Decision making
- How to say no
- Change

As this list suggests, there's more to healthy values than physical health. Partisans need to improve themselves, not only nutritionally, but psychologically, emotionally, and spiritually.

If you were stranded on a desert island with only one book, jot down which one it would be and why.
At a very low point in my life in Las Vegas, I picked up a book by Gail Sheehy entitled *Passages*. One of the main premises of the book, was that when there are crises in our lives, that's the time to make life-changing decisions and act on them. I was inspired by the book. Had I not read it, no telling how long I would've wallowed in my self-pity. Instead, I rented out my house, gave away my business, sold or gave away all my furniture, and moved back to Barstow with my mother. This example didn't improve my life. I simply went from a three and a half year methadone addiction to the chronic use of methamphetamine for four years. There's probably other books I'd rather read if I was stranded on a desert island, but *passages* is the one that comes to mind for inculcating change.

Put in writing your imaginal dialogues during this stage of your development.

By the time partisans get to this point in their recovery, they will have hopefully instituted imaginal dialogues into their everyday existence. It wasn't hard for me to do because I was talking to myself when I was alone anyway. I just had to learn how to use the concept in such a way that I could learn something from doing it, rather than blabbering about insignificant topics.

If you had only one week to live with unlimited resources, write down whom you would prefer to be with, and how you would pass the time.

Hopefully the answer to this is considerably different that the answer would've been had it been asked at the beginning of the recovery process. I would choose to be around my daughter and grandkids, but everybody don't have families that they'd want to be around. This is the chance for partisans to put in writing what they would do if they were financially able to spend time with the family members of their choice or others that mean something to them.

Write a detailed account of what you would like your obituary to say.

Here's what I want my obituary to say.

"John Smethers was the quintessence of manhood—scaling walls and crushing stone to him was mere children's play. He was known to remodel international airports on his lunch breaks, rendering them air-conditionally more efficient. He translated ethnic malapropisms for visiting dignitaries and covert innuendo for Puerto Rican immigrants. He wrote award-winning operas, and practiced time-management to perfection.

John impressed women with his sensuous and godlike demeanor. He could pedal bicycles up very steep hills with inexhaustible speed, and he could hurl rocks at distances of five miles with precision accuracy. He was an expert in carpentry, masonry, and drywall, and he was an infamous outlaw in South America.

John single-handedly tamed biker bars in big cities. He played eleven musical instruments. He was sought by the Los Angeles Dodgers, and was the subject of numerous documentaries, which includes his expertise on the air velocity of Australian Swallows. When he was bored, he built large suspension bridges, and he enjoyed hang gliding over the Grand Canyon. On Saturdays, after studying the complete works of Shakespeare and Carl Jung, he repaired toys for children free of charge.

John has sculpted celebrities and painted sunsets in the Netherlands. He was a mind reader, an honest bookie, and a card sharp. Professionals the world over drooled over his original line of evening attire. He didn't perspire, and he holds the world championship for arm wrestling. He wasn't a celebrity, yet he received fan mail.

John batted 400 with the Brooklyn Dodgers. His elegant floral arrangements earned him fame in international botany circles. Children loved and trusted him unconditionally. He could hurl boomerangs at small moving objects with precision accuracy. He once read *The Rise and Fall of the Confederate Government, Moby Dick*, and various works of Old English in one day, and still had time to remodel an entire dining room in Beverly Hills that evening. He knows the exact location of every food item in all major supermarkets. He has performed several covert operations with the CIA, FBI and the DEA, and has talked to the elephant.

John slept just once a week for twenty minutes in a chair. While on vacation in Mexico, he successfully negotiated with a group of terrorists. The laws of physics did not apply to him. He swam the Atlantic ocean and didn't get wet. The Rocky Mountains fell on his ass and he wasn't dead yet. He could look up a cow's ass and tell you the price of butter, and occasionally, to let off steam, he participated in full-contact Karate. He won bullfights in Tijuana, snow-skiing competitions in the Alps, and he spoke seven languages fluently. John sung in operas and played Hamlet on Broadway and has performed triple bypass surgery."

Please, be more realistic than this. I was simply entering some humor into all of this.

≈ X ≈

STAGE TEN

SPIRITUAL REBIRTH, HELPING OTHERS AND THE THIRD CONIUNCTIO

For many partisans, a spiritual rebirth is an integral part of the recovery process, but it's not something that needs to be worked on. It's just something that sometimes happens. Reaching out to help others in their recovery is, however, something that needs to be worked on. Partisans need to make the effort to help others (1) because people learn when they teach, and (2) because partisans need to feel like they're worth something, and helping others achieves that.

I did a research project while earning my PhD. I chose spiritual experience as a research topic, and interviewed recovered addicts and alcoholics, some of which were friends, with a variety of these experiences. I collected them over the course of a summer. I found that the range of these experiences is from a simple realization that change had to take place in order for recovery to ensue, to bright lights and ecstatic feelings, to revelations with God.

To learn what I wanted to know, I asked my research subjects to share their spiritual experiences. Those who were friends, I went to their homes. Though most of my research was collected in Barstow, I also ventured to other communities in the high desert.

For most of my life, I have been somewhat of an iconoclast because I don't recognize a traditional God figure or higher power. During my attendance in 12-step meetings over the first several years of my recovery, I only had a vague understanding of what was meant when people talked about spiritual experiences. I was aware of various perceptions of God, for 12-steppers believe that they can develop a God of their own understanding, and I was also aware of religious experiences such as the burning bush described in the Book of Exodus. I limited my interactions with recovered alcoholics and drug addicts to one request: that they explain a spiritual awakening or experience that was conducive to their recovery?

Rather than going into a discourse in hermeneutics, I will offer some definitions. The *Webster's* definition for spiritual is: "1. of the spirit or the soul. 2. of sacred matters; religious." We have a slight ambiguity here differentiating between religious and secular. Another definition concerning a spiritual phenomenon, Durkheim says: "the human mind has no need of properly scientific education to notice that there are definite sequences and a constant order of succession between phenomena *or to notice that this order is often disturbed.*" [italics mine] Most of us can agree with Webster's definition of religious or religion, which is, "a set of beliefs concerning the nature and purpose of the universe, esp. when considered as the creation of a superhuman agency."

Mysticism as defined by Webster is: "the doctrine of an immediate spiritual intuition of truths, or of a direct, intimate union of the soul with God through contemplation or spiritual ecstasy." Here again we have an ambiguity between spiritual and mystical.

William James stated that "the words 'mysticism' and 'mystical' are often used as terms of mere reproach, to throw at any opinion which we regard as vague and vast and sentimental, and without a base in either facts or logic." I am not inclined to use the definitions of others, there's too many and they're too ambiguous.

Everything just discussed and defined concerning spiritual, religious, or mystical is really phenomenology, which is a philosophy or method of inquiry based on the premise that reality consists of objects and events as they are perceived or understood in human consciousness and not of anything independent of human consciousness.

I suggest that the following testimonies be considered from the presenters' own-world orientation and consciousness, which is that of the recovery movement. I will differentiate whether these disclosures are spiritual awakenings, spiritual experiences, religious experiences, or mystical experiences. Spiritual experiences, will consist of synchronicities (unlikely but meaningful coincidences) and other phenomenon that doesn't include religion or God. Spiritual awakenings will be that of the educational variety or a realization, which doesn't include religious aspects or God. Religious experiences will always have an element of religion or God. A mystical experience will consist of experiences that *include* some kind of dialogue or interaction with a higher power, together with a usually radical or otherworldly phenomenon. A mystical category can also be indistinct or nebulous. Keep in mind, however, in the real world--especially around 12-step meetings, the terms *spiritual awakening* and *spiritual experience* are interchangeable. Because there was such a wide variety of experiences, I was compelled to separate them for this research study.

The following experiences are what Carl Jung considered to be 'spiritual'.

Jim: My friend Jim said that it "was not so much a spiritual experience, but a realization that there had to be some kind of change in order for me to go on living." He said that this took place when he took a trip to Death Valley. He wanted to take the tour at *Scotty's Castle*, but he also needed a drink, so only having money to do one or the other, he "bought a bottle and walked up to

Death Valley Scotty's grave and sat there and talked to a dead man for almost two hours." Then he told Scotty what he wanted his life to be like, asking him what he should do to achieve this. When Jim walked away from the grave, he had made a decision to change. What makes this a spiritual experience for Jim, is that he once told himself that "I'll get clean when hell freezes over." Ironically, it was snowing in Death Valley--the lowest elevation in the United States and a place that hardly ever snows. He had to take a circuitous route home because he was snowed in. Jim had a symbolic experience of hell freezing over in Death Valley. He said, "it was like a sign to me." Jim had a spiritual awakening that was characterized by a meaningful coincidence, and he has been clean and sober since.

Stan: This young man was a traveler on his way to Alabama. Stan explained that when he was at his bottom, "drinking every day, drinking vodka for breakfast, and after two unsuccessful suicide attempts, I still did not have any realization about God. I could not come to believe." Being very close to his grandmother until she passed away, he prayed to *her* rather than God. In desperation while in a blackout, he said that "she appeared to me," and he asked her: "How do I go on living life, Grandma?" Her reply was: "Service to other people." Stan said "I don't know whether that was an alcoholic hallucination or a spiritual experience, but it opened my eyes, and I have since been of service to other people whenever I can." Though he did mention God, his experience was with the spirit of his deceased grandmother. Stan, the way I see it, had a spiritual experience.

Larry: Some of the stories generated here as spiritual experiences are similar to some experiences written by William James in *The Varieties of Religious Experience*. This holds true with Larry. His experience happened right after an argument with his wife. Driving into Barstow from him and his family's rural home, Larry had "the most profound feeling of love I have ever had. It was not just for a couple seconds either. It lasted for a long time. As I was driving, this energy was generating out of myself and my truck. It was unbelievable." Larry said that he had never, before or since, experienced anything like it. Larry's paroxysm is common in the celestial sphere of spiritual experiences.

William James said "it may come gradually, or it may occur abruptly; it may come through altered feelings, or through altered powers of action; or it may come through new intellectual insights." James also said that a new birth may be away from religion into incredulity; or it may be from moral scrupulosity into freedom and license; or it may be produced by the irruption into the individual's life of some new stimulus or passion, such as *love*, [Larry's experience] or ambition. In these instances we have precisely the same psychological form of event--a firmness, stability, and equilibrium succeeding a period of storm and stress and inconsistency [Larry's quarrel with his wife]. Larry and I agree that he had a spiritual experience.

<u>Terry</u>: This woman's experience was different. It happened gradually over a period of roughly two years. It started when the dysfunctional relationship she was in ended. Though she continued to use drugs, she was still having an ongoing experience. She sent her experience to me by email. I will quote it in its entirety:

> The part of the whole experience that really impressed me as being "miraculous" was the recovery process that went on, unbeknownst to me for the two years between "turning it over" and first walking through the doors of AA. The totality of events are too lengthy to include, but the fact that I had literally done every step in the program before I had ever seen them, seems like way more than a coincidence.
>
> The depression, desperation, and realization that "it wasn't working" was the First Step: "I realized that I was powerless over my addiction and that my life had become unmanageable."
>
> The preceding years of spiritual studies had led up to Step Two: "came to believe that a power greater than myself could restore me to sanity." This was like a split-second thing that almost immediately segued into Step Three: "made the decision to turn my will and life over to the care of God as I understood Him." The talk I had with God (this was a real discussion, by the way), was the beginning of this step for me, walking out the door was the culmination of it.
>
> The Fourth Step: "made a searching and fearless moral inventory of ourselves" was an ongoing process that spanned the entire two years. I looked at every inch, every nook, every cranny of what made up "me." I didn't like what I saw very much. Then I started writing down all the things about me that I knew--the good stuff, the bad stuff. The childhood and adolescent shit that you don't tell anybody. How I felt about it. What I thought was real, what I thought was imagined, and how all of those experiences, real or perceived, were affecting me. It was, I suppose, an extended attempt at self-analyzation.
>
> Step Five: "admitted to God, to ourselves, and to another human being the exact nature of our wrongs" was another drawn out process. The "other human being" was any MF who would listen to me. I was on a Mission. I wanted everybody I knew to know just exactly what a rotten, no-good, person I had become and why. I was really tired of hiding things. And I really had a "burning desire" to help other people not to make the same mistakes or to

feel like they were the only "bad guys in town."

Step Six: "became willing to have God remove all these defects of character." Well, duh...

Step Seven: "humbly asked God to remove my shortcomings." This I did, also. Probably several times. I'm still doing this step today.

Step Eight: "made a list of all the persons that we had harmed, and became willing to make amends to them all." I don't know that I listed "all" the people, but I did list many of them, including what I had done to hurt them.

Step Nine: "made direct amends wherever possible" was just the natural outgrowth of having made the list in the first place, so I started doing that whenever I had the chance.

Step Ten: "Continued to take personal inventory and when I was wrong, promptly admitted it." Again, this was just a natural extension of Step Four, and I was still on that Mission.

Step Eleven: "sought through prayer and meditation to improve my conscious contact with God as I understand Him." He IS my life, was then, is now.

Step Twelve: "having had a spiritual awakening as a result of these steps, we tried to carry this message to addicts, and to practice these principles in all our affairs." Absolutely–I was still on my mission. I had developed "rigorous honesty" to a fault. I was out to save the world, and share this miraculous spiritual gift I had been given.

Maybe my story doesn't have the allure of "bright lights" and spectral visitation, but it is the truth, and it has forever changed my life.

Terry's experience is difficult to catagorize, but early in her message she made the statement, "The talk I had with God (this was a real discussion, by the way), was the beginning of this step for me, walking out the door was the culmination of it." Having that one small element of God in comparison to the entire experience places Terry's experience in the category of spiritual experience, mainly because of its profound synchronicity. Synchronicity was defined by Jung as an acausal connecting principle, an essentially mysterious connection between the personal psyche and the material worked, based on the fact that at bottom they are only different forms of energy.

<u>Cheryl</u>: After breaking up with her husband, Cheryl moved in with her mom in San Diego. She had been drinking heavily. Cheryl and her mom often had violent quarrels after being around each other for a while; therefore, she started looking for her own apartment. When she had collected an entire page of phone numbers and addresses, she started making calls. When she was "about half way down the page, I dialed a number, and the person on the other end said *'Alcoholic's Anonymous.'* I was really shocked, and I hung the phone up. It was a wrong number--I just knew it was." A couple weeks later, Cheryl's husband came for a visit. He seemed so clean and calm, "and I wanted to know how he did that." She explained that "I'd been acting really crazy, and he told me to go to AA. I thought, 'wow,' maybe I would because he'd been clean for about nine months. He looked so clean and calm. He had something that I wanted to have. I was drinking a lot of wine and being really crazy, and fighting with everybody." After her husband left, she started thinking: "I wonder if this could really be it." Then she started looking for that paper with all the numbers on it. "I found it and I talked to this guy. He told me that it sounds like your life is unmanageable." At this point Cheryl laughed and said "today I know what that means, but then I thought 'how does that guy know--how does he know my life is unmanageable?'" She started going to meetings, and about two weeks later she wondered how this happened, "so I went back to where I wrote that number down, and when I looked at the paper, I had switched two numbers. So, because of looking for an apartment and switching those two numbers because I'm dyslexic, I found *Alcoholic's Anonymous*." Cheryl was sober sixteen years when I interviewed her. This is another spiritual experience, not because of a coincidence, but because of a mistake.

<u>Harold</u>: Harold's experience is what would be considered by many as religious, and I must agree. Abstinent from the use of any chemical substances for approximately sixty days, Harold was "incapable of eating, was bleeding internally, vomiting and crapping blood, and having nose bleeds for sixteen days. I had lost a lot of weight." He had also been breaking out with sores caused from herpes, which he had for some time. At this point he was experiencing incomprehensible demoralization: "crying, hurting, and had enough, and feeling like I was going to die." He said that he lied down on the floor and looked up and said, "fuck it; fuck it God, help me. Please, if there's anything there either heal me or kill me. I can't take it anymore." He then said with emphasis "that no sooner had 'more' come out of my mouth, a light hit me and encompassed my whole body, and I was immediately raised above my body with still full control of my senses. I could hear my body behind me crying--whimpering. It was inside of this light. It was just this overwhelming sense of peace and ease. It was a place that I've never been able to get into words." The only thing that Harold's doppelganger experience could compare to, he said, "was that of a hundred thousand orgasms. As I was above my body, this wind and light kind of blew through me, and at that moment I knew that I would never have to use drugs or drink alcohol again. I actually heard a voice saying

that I was healed, and that if I ever had the opportunity to tell this story, to tell it." He then explained the process of coming back into his body with the light, wind and sensations disappearing into a halcyon of inner peace. After that, Harold said, "the way I could see was different, everything around me seemed to be glowing. It seemed like I could actually see the atomic structure of air for a few moments, then the very next thought was that I flipped out." Then his overwhelming experience was over and he went to sleep. When he awoke the next morning, he remembered the experience, and acknowledged that he still felt different, and had no desire for drugs and alcohol. The most astonishing part of this story is that Harold was not bleeding anymore. Also, from that day on, he has not suffered any symptoms from herpes. He suffered monthly sores and lesions from herpes from 1986 until this happened in 1990, and since then there is not a trace after having gotten biyearly checkups for at least two years. Harold had what I consider a religious experience because what he went through had elements that *included* some kind of dialogue or interaction with God, but the more extraordinary element was that it also consisted of a radical other-worldly phenomenon, which could arguably be placed in the mystical category.

Michele: Here is another one that was emailed to me. Michele is a woman who I used to drink and use drugs with in Barstow. Her story is quoted in its entirety from Las Cruces, New Mexico:

> When I first moved here to get sober I didn't have much money and no friends. Thanksgiving was here and I wanted to go to the Arid Club to eat a free turkey dinner. I had saved two Kennedy silver half dollars from all my drugging in Barstow, because I loved Kennedy. I had enough gas in the truck to get to the club but I didn't have enough to get home. I figured God would surely want me to spend Thanksgiving with other people and eat good, but what about the gas? I prayed and ask God to give me the gas money home from the club. But, just in case I took my Kennedy half dollars. I only needed a dollars worth of gas. Anyway, I got to the club and sat in a chair watching all the people mill about. Every time someone would pass by me, I would think "there goes a dollar." I told myself not to ask anyone, to wait for God to supply my need. I sat there for about twenty minutes when this guy came over to me and asked me if I needed any money. My mouth fell open and I looked up and smiled. I told this man yes, I did need money. He gave me a dollar twenty-five. By waiting twenty minutes I got 25 cents more than I would have asked for myself. This particular incident has caused me to believe, and when I get in doubt these days, I can recall the miracle. Some years later I was sharing about this incident and this woman found it touching. Every year on my sobriety date she gave me another Kennedy half dollar.

Michele having included God in her disclosure, places it in the religious experience category. Some experiences are graced with bright lights and celestial voices, but experiences on the opposite end of the spectrum can be just as meaningful to those who had them.

<u>Tom</u>: Tom and a friend went to a man's house to see if they could be of help. They tried getting the man into any treatment facility from Covina to Corona to San Bernardino. They were left with only one more place to go in Upland. "It so happened that this was Dennis Kneivel--Evel Kneivel's brother. They had two locked doors at this hospital, and somehow we walked right through them. We were standing by the cubicle where the nurses were. They turned around and said that 'there is no way you guys could have walked through those doors. How did you get in here?' We just explained to her that we just opened the door and walked in, and that it was the last place we had to go. They wouldn't believe us at first. They looked around and there wasn't anybody else there but us." Fortunately, they admitted Dennis into the hospital. Tom said "I do not know how long he stayed sober or what, it makes no difference, but that was a major spiritual experience in my life." Evidently the lock mechanism couldn't be opened from the outside with a key, and there were only a couple people there close enough and they didn't open it from the inside. Spiritual experiences consist of synchronicities (unlikely but meaningful coincidences) and other phenomenon that doesn't include religion or God. I believe Tom placed it in the appropriate category.

<u>Mike</u>: He shared with me that "it was my second night out of detox at BMC. As I was trying to sleep, and I was going over in my head how I was going to 'trick' the system again so I could continue living the way I was accustomed-- i.e., drinking a twelve-pack every night at least." Mike had already said his usual prayers--"I've always done that--as well as a couple new ones they taught me at BMC. Then, all of a sudden, there was like a bright light in my head and a voice that wasn't my mine talking to me (i.e., outside of me) that said, 'trust me, with me you can do it.'" Mike said that "as soon as it had come, it was gone," and then he asked himself, "What was that?" Upon realizing it was not "my thinking," he thought that maybe what he's been hearing about how a higher power could help him, "and how I can't do it alone, cause that's what I was thinking when it happened--how I was gonna get myself through this one." Since then his cravings are gone and he has not had the desire to drink or use again. That was eight years prior to this interview, which was in 2001. Did Mike have a mystical, religious, or a spiritual experience? Since he didn't specifically mention religion or God, I place it with spiritual experiences.

<u>Jackie</u>: Jackie's son was in the hospital. He had been clean and sober about two years, but his recovery was tenuous. Before leaving the hospital during a visit, little Jack asked his dad: "Am I going to have to worry about you drinking and using now?" Jackie assured him that he had no need to worry. How confident

he was inside with how he answered his son's question, was also tenuous. However, Jackie's confidence was solidified when his son passed away a week later. What could be worse than losing a son or daughter? Admittedly, Jackie would have probably lost his sobriety date had his son not died. The reason Jackie considers this a spiritual experience, and I agree, is that his recovery would not have been sustained if he had not assured little Jack otherwise.

Gina: Gina's opprobrium had been disappointing her two kids for years, and she would not come to terms with the humiliation she found herself in resulting from her addiction. She went to treatment *again*. After she was there for a while, it somehow occurred to her that she was admitted to the rehab on her son's birthday; What a revelation! She had many previous sobriety dates, some from rehabs and some from NA, but this one was special. After being released after six and a half months, she held onto her recovery, sometimes by just a thread. That thread was her clean date. She said that her recovery probably would not have lasted had she not had this supposed "coincidence" to hang on to. Like Jackie, Gina had a spiritual experience, contingent on the love of a son, that kept her clean and sober after disappointing her kids so many times before.

Up to this time the experiences I have collected have been in some way related to their recovery from addiction. The following experience is from an AA member, but the experience is not connected to his drinking and subsequent recovery. I don't remember for sure, but I might have neglected to inform him beforehand that I was collecting experiences that were connected in some way to recovery. Or, I might have just wanted to include it because it was so inexplicable.

Gilbert: This man, who was in his seventies at the time, told me that he was driving a truck up a mountain for his employer. The truck broke down, and it was getting dark. He said that he "could hear the birds and the wind, and see the trees and the stars in the sky. It was a beautiful night, you know." There wasn't much traffic, so Gilbert asked himself, "What am I going to do? So I decided to pray. 'God,' I said, 'I know that you exist, I know you're real, that you're taking care of me, and I know you made the heavens and everything that is here. I am alone here. If you would, do something to let me know you're really here.'" After praying, he looked out of the truck window at the stars, but focused on only one. He stared at the one star for a while, then noticed "that it was getting closer." The closer the star got, the brighter everything around him was getting, especially illuminating "the whole truck." He said, "What is happening to me? It's getting closer and brighter." Being confused--not scared he told me, he got on the floorboard. By the time he looked up, "it was only about ten feet away. It was so bright that it was like being inside of a lightbulb--even brighter, so bright that it was blinding me." Nothing more happened while the star was still there, but after it left, "I noticed something: I couldn't hear the birds or the wind no more. The whole world stood still. Not a sound. Then I realized that God was showing me what I had asked of him." Gilbert's religious experience was mystical.

Before I conclude the experiences, I want to establish a common thread that goes through a majority of them. Remember Larry, who said "I had the most profound feeling of love I ever had."And Harold, the one who left his body? Mike, who heard a voice that wasn't his own? And then Gilbert who experienced the bright light when his truck broke down. Also, there's…

Leah: She shared with me that when her life was totally out of control at six years sober she put off getting a bottle till the next day, and that night in bed she had an overwhelming sense of peace and warmth, accompanied with an inner assurance that she would not ever have to drink or use again.

Pat: As he was driving home one afternoon, he "was passing an old barn on top of a hill overlooking a valley below. Suddenly, the colors of the day and the pastoral scene became vivid. There was a feeling of a tuning fork being struck. The vibrations seemed to fill all my senses and for the first time in a long time, I realized I was alive and a party to the beauty around me. This all happened in an instant but my memory of this is vivid with the ability to recall the scene and the vibration at anytime. It seemed to be a coming in tune with the universe."

Lawrence: He told me about sitting on his bed when a bright light and a warm feeling came over him. His experience was brief but profound, one that he said he would never forget.

The most common threads running through most of these *spiritual* experiences are the feelings of peace, warmth, love, etc., also bright lights of varying degrees and kinds, and of voices of which were not necessarily always with God. The rest of them were not as relative, but definitely unique and fascinating.

My previous ignorance concerning spiritual experience has changed into more of an understanding than I was asking for. I've realized that spiritual awakening, religious and mystical experiences, can be placed under the umbrella term, spiritual experience; however, one can also isolate spiritual experience in any way they choose without using the terminology or the defined categories I have presented here. A good example would be Gina, who went into treatment on her son's birthday. A more common description of Gina's spiritual experience would be a simple coincidence. Considering Gina's experience as spiritual has enabled me to label a similar spiritual experience; however, until this data collection, I never thought of it as that. About nine months after my release from prison, I was visiting my daughter and her husband. We were talking about clean dates. I mentioned that mine was May 7th. She looked at me and said, "I really haven't put much emphasis on my date, but that date rings a bell." She dug around in some drawers and came out with a piece of paper with the same date on it! We shared the warmth of the moment and each of us carried the information in our own ways. I've stayed clean and sober, and I probably would have anyway, and maybe that's why I didn't consider it a spiritual experience; perhaps more of a significant awakening. Since it's possible that it helped sustain my recovery, at least for a period of time, I simply refer to it now as a meaningful experience.

After I collected these experiences, I came to realize that my project was limited. The scope of the spiritual experiences I collected was limited to the confines of recovered or recovering addicts and alcoholics. I am also aware that the *scope* of spiritual experiences I selected is also limited. For example, the religious denominations and the multitude of people within them, undoubtedly have many variations of religious experiences--not to mention many other kinds of mystical experiences. Also, the sample population that contributed to my project is also limited in ways: geography, nationality or ethnicity, cultural differences within those groups, plus religious and educational backgrounds. I will not elaborate further on the many ways my research was limited; however, regardless of the limitations, I have answered my original question, which was: what is a spiritual experience?

But what is most important, how has my research contributed to the *anima mundi*? How I lacked the knowledge, or at least a working definition of spiritual experience, I can only speculate. If this were the case with me, how many others attending 12-step meetings are just as ignorant or confused? Whereas my ignorance did not cause me to return to active addiction, it could have. What if Gina would not have noticed the coincidence of being admitted into treatment on her son's birthday? She told me what would have happened, as it had so many times before. Would Jackie had stayed clean if his dying son had not asked if he had to worry about his dad drinking and using anymore? Jackie knows the answer to that question. I have only touched on some of the experiences that have been conducive to recovery for many; therefore, if partisans learn the nature and importance of spiritual experiences, maybe then they will be able to recognize them when they happen. Those whose recovery is just starting, has a lot on their minds, and having spiritual experiences could well sound quite ridiculous in early recovery unless it can be explained in a way that is palatable to them.

My present life would not be as abstinent as it is had I not, for purely selfish reasons, volunteered for a substance abuse education program (Project Change) when I was in prison. Who could've told a philistine like me that a prison sentence would be the best thing that would happen to me in my entire life?

Put in writing how you've helped another recovering addict, then describe the situation and how it felt to you.

Sponsorship in 12-step programs is one way to reach out. Speaking at schools and other institutions about recovery is also a good one. Getting certified as a drug and alcohol counselor is even better. For the sake of this assignment, partisans can start by writing about helping in small ways, like favors for other recovering addicts. Helping in bigger ways can come later unless opportunities present themselves.

Discuss on paper how you usually handle various types of conflict, and any ways that you can think of to be more effective in conflict resolution.
Conflict resolution is a wide range of methods of addressing sources of conflict, and of finding means of resolving a given conflict or of continuing it in fewer destructive forms. Processes of conflict resolution generally include negotiation, mediation, diplomacy and creative peace building.

Do you want to become an drug and alcohol counselor? Write down the reasons why or why not.
Some partisans will be attracted to the idea, but others won't. When I finished my bachelors degree, I started a degree program in marriage and family counseling, but dropped out because I wasn't willing to jump all the hurdles it required to become one. My way has been through writing books and with a presence on the Internet.

Write down how much time you are willing to devote to working with others in their recovery.
My uncle Orvil was drunk for 50 years, and then got sober. His way of helping drunks was to let them live with him until they could get on their feet. More often than not, however, he had to ask them to leave because of drunkenness.

Once the ten stages of development are complete, partisans need to start the process of the third coniunctio, which can take several years. Partisans will determine when individuation of the alchemical process of recovery has been achieved. At that point, the content of the alchemical vessel has turned into Gold. They have become the philosopher's stone. Again, the alchemical imagery and processes will continue to be used, and hopefully the partisan will also have found a life worth living and an enduring interest in the spiritual aspects of recovery, of alchemical transformation, and in the spiritual aspects of alchemy, which can be a tool for spiritual growth for the rest of their lives. This is the time when the final rite of passage has been started, and it must be an undertaking that can nourish serenity for the rest of the partisan's life.

The rites of the third coniunctio aren't, like the first and second ones, a one-time thing. For some, it'll take longer than for others. Partisans can repeat what they did in the second coniunctio, like vison quests, where the partisan spends a week alone in the mountains or desert away from civilization; but this time they do it every six months or year, or however often they believe they need to. Or, a day of fasting every week every six months for a year. Writing a book is a good one. Whatever it is, it must be something that eventually elevates partisans to a level that they are not willing to give up *no matter what*! Keep in mind, partisan proclivities toward addiction will always be there. The philosopher's stone doesn't translate to cured.

A common plan for those in early recovery is earning a certificate or degree in drug and alcohol studies. What better way for partisans to embark on the third coniunctio than to pursue a livelihood in the helping professions? For those who haven't achieved any higher education, a certificate in alcohol and drug counseling is a two-year certificate program in most schools that offer it. For those with AA degrees, there are BAs in the field of drug and alcohol studies, as well as MAs and PhDs. If partisans are already ensconced in a high paying profession, another part-time professional endeavor in counseling other addicts would definitely contribute to the *anima mundi* and achieve the philosopher's stone at the same time.

While I was working on my doctorate, I had a full time job for the federal government, but I also held a part-time position at a state mandated DUI school where I did groups and counseled alcoholics and addicts who'd been convicted of DUI. It was only four hours a week in the evenings, so it didn't interfere with school or my day job. Today I write books like this to keep me connected and do my part in contributing to the *anima mundi*.

In early recovery when I was a student at the community college level, I took a 22-mile bicycle ride every morning. During those rides, I often thought about what fun it would be to take a ride from somewhere around the California/Oregon border down highway 101 to somewhere around Santa Barbara. I never found the time to do it, but if I'd been going through the alchemical process of recovery at the time, this would've been ideal for the third coniunctio, except I would've done it every six months for five years.

I realize that many partisans aren't going to have the time it takes for some of my suggestions, but others will. The ones that don't have the time, will have to come up with ideas on their own. It doesn't matter what it is as long as it's something ambitious that can be done periodically over a period of years. Who knows, some partisans might like it so much that they continue doing it for the rest of their lives. What a great way to celebrate a brand new clean and sober life.

THINKING PATTERNS

Addicts don't think like normal people, so let's explore the thinking of partisans to get a better understanding of how they think, and learn why they need to monitor and discipline their thought processes.

Critical thinking is purposeful, reasoned and goal directed. It is thinking and knowledge and the relationship between them. The ability to plan, be flexible, tenacious, and the willingness to self-correct are the characteristics of critical thinking essential for those in recovery to learn.

Critical thinking cannot be spontaneous. We don't get up in the morning and think our way through brushing our teeth and getting dressed, because we do those things by habit. Partisans bring many of their old behaviors into recovery with them, and spontaneity, in the form of hasty decisions, are common. Critical thinking involves the use of cognitive functions, such as memory, reasoning, decision making, problem solving, and creativity.

Memory: A good definition for memory is the faculty or process of retaining or recalling past experiences. There are many mnemonic devices to aid memory, and most partisans will concede that they have lost a portion of that ability that was previously available to them. Acrostics are sentences created by words that begin with the first letters of a series of words. For example, "Every good boy does fine," is the music student's acrostic for recalling the notes associated with the lines of a treble clef staff--EGBDF. Another one that normies might use when balking about drug addicts moving into or living in their neighborhood is NIMBY (not in my back yard). Rhymes and songs like the McDonald's song, "Nobody can do it like _____ can." Or how about, twiddely dee, twiddely dum, gimmy your dope or I'll get my gun. The loci system is also a good one, which uses visual associations with locations already known. The peg system is another. It uses key words represented by numbers; for example, one is a gun, two is a crew, three is a knee. The phonetic system is similar, but instead of words representing numbers, sounds do. If partisans employ these methods, they'll inevitably improve their memories; however, unlearning long ingrained habits is difficult to do, especially when there is no incentive. Partisans are often discriminated against, which is why they will think such thoughts as, "Why even try? What good will it do?"

What is usually referred to as forgetting is either the inability to recall stored information or the failure to store information in the first place. Addicts, especially practicing ones, have selective memory syndrome, the failure to store information in the first place. The addict's attitude is, if the information isn't of any immediate use, then why make the effort to remember it?

I read somewhere about another memory technique that a man invented when he was a kid. He said that when he went places with his parents in the car, one of the ways he'd spend time was to look at signs along the highway; for example, he saw a SHELL oil company sign, then he wondered what that word would look like in alphabetical order, and he came up with EHLLS. There's no specific purpose for this example, but it's a good way for partisans, or anybody for that matter, to exercise their brain. The brain is a muscle, and like any other muscle, it should be exercised.

Psychologist Gordon Allport showed research participants a picture of a white man with a knife holding up a black man with a suit. This picture was presented in a flash to test the accuracy of eyewitness testimony in a situation in which racial prejudice might influence their perception. How memory can be influenced by biases, prejudices, and stereotypes should lead people to question themselves periodically. The same scenario, of course, could be substituted with a man in a suit holding up a younger man with facial hair, long scraggly hair or a bald head, with tattoos on his arms and neck--the stereotypical jointster. Xenophobia (the hatred or fear of groups different from oneself) and discrimination aren't restricted to ethnic groups. Partisans often deal with it in diverse ways. I know I have.

Reasoning: Most people, especially addicts, don't use the same psychological processes in finding conclusions required by the laws of formal logic or reasoning. Biases, prejudices and emotions are some of the reasons why this is so. The idea of someone reasoning irrationally is known as a result of the acceptance of categorical syllogisms for assessing beliefs and attitudes. It's a common conclusion with categorical syllogisms that people untrained at reasoning are not logical in their inferences, and that they usually base their decisions on personal knowledge, prejudices, and biases.

Normies will base their decisions and their *observations* primarily on personal knowledge and biases when associating drug use with appearances. Jointsters can usually identify other jointsters, and not from the stereotypical observations such as shaved heads, tattoos, long hair, or their attire. Anybody can do that. I'm talking about a look, an often very subtle look that's in their countenance, their walk, the way they carry themselves. All the other stereotypical nuances may not even be there, but a Jointster can *generally* recognize a fellow jointster without the more obvious nuances being present.

Addicts are very adept at manipulation and persuasion; therefore, most of them don't believe they can be bamboozled (ya can't con a con). They're wrong about that because they're basing their decisions primarily on personal knowledge and biases. They doubt that the man with the 'normie' appearance is capable of hoodwinking them, and rarely will they admit when it happens. Here's some different types of reasoning:

Inductive reasoning - If I have a situation where a statement has two premises, and the premises are logical, then I can find a valid conclusion through inductive reasoning.

Here's a superficial example: If every person I have ever seen is a jointster, I would use this evidence to support the conclusion that everyone in the world are jointsters. Obviously I can't be absolutely positive of this. It's always possible that someone I've never met is not a jointster. However, If I met just one person that was not a jointster, then my conclusion must be wrong. So it is with inductive reasoning, I can never prove that my conclusion is correct, but I can prove it's incorrect. Partisans often have a difficult time with inductive reasoning when it comes to dealing with people. When dealing with normies in the real world, they will often employ the same strategies or tactics that they've been using with people like themselves. And when they try to *not* do that, they end up under or overestimating whom they're dealing with, or they make an enemy, or they're ignored or ridiculed, etc.

Deductive reasoning - This type of reasoning begins with statements known or believed to be true. A simple example would be the statement, "all jointsters use drugs," then you could conclude that Lynda, a woman you've never met, also uses drugs. This is the *modus operandi* of most people, including jointsters, but they often carry it too far. For example, if I believe all jointsters are thieves, then to me it isn't being unethical to steal from other jointsters. As I've mentioned throughout this book, partisans need to continually monitor and discipline their thought processes.

Syllogistic reasoning - In a nutshell, this form of reasoning is deciding whether a conclusion can rightly be inferred from two or more statements. One type of syllogistic reasoning is categorical reasoning, which involves terms that tell us how many, like *some* or *none*.

There are several types of syllogistic reasoning, which can get recondite and technical; therefore, I'll just expand on the type cited above. I've made an effort in this work to use terminology such as some, often, many, or most, when referring to addicts, jointsters, or partisans. I can't say with assurance that all jointsters are thieves, or that all addicts are *puerile*. I've tried to deal with majorities in my examples, and if I haven't been consistent during this work, then replace my error with language that's more accurate. Anyway, this is something I've had to learn to do. Prior to recovery, which is *common* with *most* partisans, I made blanket statements. Blanket statements are *often* prejudicial statements, and I don't mean racial prejudice. Prejudice means to pre-judge, and many people prejudge jointsters by labeling them.

Probabilistic reasoning - is using information to decide that a conclusion is likely true or not. In everyday contexts, much of our reasoning is probabilistic.

Suppose I learn that people who have hepatitis C are frequently nauseous, depressed, and are lacking in energy. I then notice that I have these symptoms. Does that mean that I have hep C? It shouldn't, because those symptoms can be caused by other conditions or circumstances. However, when former intravenous drug users have these symptoms, they *should* assume they have hep C, or at least get tested for it. Given this example, it's easy enough to see how partisans could mistakenly come to conclusions based on the experiences of their addictive mind-set and lifestyle.

Thinking is often like the scientific method of hypothesis testing. A hypothesis is a set of beliefs about the nature of the world. It's usually a belief about a relationship between two or more variables. In more simpler terms, it's an educated guess. There are several methods of testing hypotheses: inductive and deductive methods through operational definitions, independent and dependent variables, measurement sensitivity, populations and samples, and variability; furthermore, there are several ways to determine cause: isolation and control of variables, prospective and retrospective research, correlation and cause (which people frequently get confused), illusory correlation, validity, and reliability. I've learned to be aware of self-fulfilling prophecies in life as well as in learning to think in a critical manner. For the most part, I accept the effectiveness of double-blind studies, depending on the merits of the research sample. In my previous life, when I wrote and called in my own medical prescriptions, I became familiar with double-blind studies while researching pharmaceutical drugs for my personal use. Through a double-blind study, for example, I learned that propoxyphene (Darvon) is less effective for pain than plain Aspirin. However, when I wanted to detox for a while, I also learned that propoxyphene was effective for treating withdrawal symptoms resulting from the physical addiction to opiate drugs. This information about Darvon is no longer valid because the drug has been discontinued. The best drug now-a-days for opiate withdrawal is Clonidine.

Decision making: Decision-making can be stressful, and it isn't limited to the uneducated: Whenever there is a simple error that ordinary people fall for, there is always a slightly more sophisticated version of the same problem that experts fall for. I didn't write scrips only for mind-altering substances. I utilized my scam to provide prescription medication for me and my family. Obviously, a physician's expertise through experience would enable him to select more appropriate drugs than I did, even though I had a working knowledge of the Physician's Desk Reference, but I did it anyway, and luckily didn't do any harm to myself or my family.

The availability heuristic is a rule of thumb we use to solve problems. For example, when I read the question about whether there were more deaths due to homicide or due to diabetes-related diseases, and then read the answer (diabetes) and the reason why (the media), something clicked in my head. I'm now more aware of the effects of publicity. The media being in our face so much with all the murder and mayhem being publicized, naturally homicide was my choice. I was also fascinated that the availability of information in our memory will frequently determine the alternative selection in a decision-making process. In early recovery, I went to a lot of 12-step meetings. Here is an example of an availability heuristic. When meeting time rolls around, sometimes people are faced with a decision: to go or not to go. Let's say the meeting I attended last night wasn't a very good one, and the availability of information in my head at the present time concerns a money-making scheme. The alternative I select stands a good chance of being the one for making money, even though I may not need money as much as what I might learn in a meeting to enhance and sustain my recovery.

Many common myths inhibit recovering addicts from taking the essential steps for sound decision making. Here are some examples.
The future is all about chance or luck, so there's no use spending a lot of time and effort trying to make the best possible decision about something that isn't really important.
This is not uncommon thinking for partisans. Also, partisans bring a lot of old thinking patterns into recovery with them, which contributes to high relapse rates. In the face of discrimination, partisans shouldn't make such blanket statements as, "What's the use of pursuing education if nobody will have anything to do with ex-cons?" The discrimination that I've encountered in trying to teach at colleges and universities, concerning my criminal background, has not in any way given me cause to regret my education. Many older jointsters say such things as, "I'm too old to go back to school." That's bullshit! Let's say Lynda is 40 years old. In four years she will be 44 years old whether she gets a bachelors degree or not. Which is better, 44 years old with or without the degree?

Asking questions about an opportunity is asking for trouble.
This myth sounds rather ridiculous; however, especially in early recovery, the thinking of partisans is muddled and they're often overwhelmed. It's like students who are afraid to ask questions because they're afraid the question will be thought of as a stupid. Most people can learn this lesson from a four-year-old boy. When I was ten years old, my mom was babysitting the little brother of one of my friends. My mom was busy doing something when she heard a bunch of racket in the kitchen. When she entered the kitchen, there sat the little guy with everything that was in the lower cupboards spread all over the floor. "Danny, you're not supposed to get into other people's things? It isn't nice." Little Danny looked up at her in earnest and said, "How me supposed to know what you got if me no look?"

Experts always agree. If you've asked one, you've asked them all.
Along with other character flaws, addicts bring sloth into early recovery, so

wouldn't it make sense to take the time and effort to do the research, rather than taking the word of one expert? Addicts aren't the only ones who can benefit from deflating this myth. Most adjunct (part time) college instructors are professionals of some kind. Many of these instructors are also educated know-it-alls. I call the educated know-it-all 'the sage on the stage.' They'll stand up there and spew out information like it was indisputable, and much of their *performance* is an egotistical and arrogant need to bolster their self-importance. What they often do is spew their opinions as facts along with legitimate facts. I use educators as examples because I witnessed this in academia. So yes, deflate this myth and get a second or third opinion. The sage on the stage isn't always right.

I'll turn this around onto partisans. The prisons are full of jailhouse lawyers, some deservedly so, but most not. The knowledge that these jointsters profess to have is usually just as egotistical and arrogant as the sage on the stage. They're not only jailhouse lawyers, but they're jailhouse psychologists, sociol-ogists, anthropologists, and every other kind of ist, and they bring all of that with them when they hit the streets. *Understanding* jointsters is fraught with paradox, ambivalence, contradiction, and uncertainty. They often have inflated egos who also think of themselves as scumbags. Some consciously feel about themselves in this way, which translates into diminished self worth. Or, it can be unconscious, and then it usually manifests in behavior that will get them back in the joint.

Consulting non-experts is pointless.

Whom are you going to trust, a drug and alcohol counselor with one or two years of education who is a recovered addict, or a normie with a Ph.D. in clinical psychology who isn't a recovered addict or alcoholic? All the education that the Ph.D. has, is of little comfort to recovering addicts. Not that normies with clinical degrees aren't qualified to do the job, but the vast majority of addicts are more comfortable with those who have a background similar to theirs.

Also, professionals who are enmeshed in their own fields of expertise, are often hard pressed to look outside of the box of their discipline for innovative ideas. When looking for answers in their own discipline, it's often more productive to ask those who are far removed from that discipline for ideas or answers. A plumber might come up with an insight that the psychologist is overlooking because the psychologist can get trapped inside of a psychological mind-set.

If everyone in your group of decision-makers agree on the same choice, you can feel secure that it is a sound decision.

If it's a 12-step group, be aware that 12-step groups are not hot-beds of mental health. They're addicts who, and like everybody else, they make mistakes and often agree with each other. When I first started going to meetings after being released from prison, there was a highly respected man with 30 years of sobriety who used to say, "you can't think your way to good living, you have to live your way to good thinking." I'd been taught that we need to monitor and discipline our thoughts to change the way we live, which would equate to 'thinking your way to good living.' Well, a lot of people heard him say that it's better to 'live your way to good thinking,' and so it started getting parroted at meetings all over the area by others. He made believers out of many, especially the ones he sponsored and the ones they sponsored.

Sometimes we need to challenge the status quo. When teaching college courses, I encouraged my students to challenge the status quo, to challenge even what I said (but don't get carried away), and even challenge what's in the text books. That is how innovation occurs. Those who operate on nothing but present knowledge, often stagnate.

Commitments are always irrevocable.

This one can be easily misunderstood. As long as partisans are not making a *habit* of breaking commitments, which most of them were doing when they were practicing, it *is* okay to break commitments once in a while if plenty of notice is given. It's not okay to leave people hanging or call at the last minute and cancel.

Problem Solving: A tendency in problem-solving, especially with addicts, is to pick the first solution that comes to mind and run with it. The disadvantage of this approach is that they may run off a cliff or into a worse problem than they started with. A better strategy to solve problems, of course, is to select the most practical option out of many.

If partisans don't have a clue how to plan, then it wouldn't do them any good for someone to tell them to plan a solution. If they can't think of solutions, then how are they going to generate and evaluate any? There are strategies that can be used to help generate solutions. All of them won't work for everybody, but learning how to use different strategies can give partisans direction for problem solving. However, some of the these strategies don't lend themselves as solutions for partisans, and others are self-explanatory. I'll give some examples.

Means-Ends Analysis - When a goal is not immediately attainable, partisans can take detours to break the problem down into smaller problems, called subproblems, each with its own goal, called subgoals.

Let's say that a concerned parent wants to help their son get out of the pits of addictive despair. This isn't an easy task, so the problem needs to be broken down into a smaller problem, say, learning about addiction first. To solve this subproblem it will be necessary to set a goal, like learning about dealing with addicts by going to Ala-non or Nar-anon, and work from there.

Simplification - A good way to approach problems is to strip away as much of the complexity as possible to reduce it to a more simple form.

When addicts attend group counseling, say in a drug rehab, they're bombarded with solutions, techniques, and strategies to help keep them in recovery when they leave. They are told that they only need to change one thing–and that's everything, but that's not going to happen overnight, so the best way to proceed is incrementally. Implement change slowly, one thing at a time, and make a conscious effort to avoid getting overwhelmed. The most common reason for people dropping out of college is getting overwhelmed with work caused by procrastination.

I worked in a drug rehab for a couple years. I used to facilitate four different groups, one of which was on nutrition. When I first started, I bombarded the clients with information because I was coming at them from an educator's perspective. I came to realize that the information I was giving them wasn't the only thing they needed. They also needed practical suggestions to use in the real world, so I started integrating suggestions along with the information, and I used my personal experiences as a tool. Implementing major change is exceptionally difficult for addicts in early recovery, because they want what they want NOW, or preferably yesterday. Anyway, I suggested that clients start with one thing, such as keeping their carbohydrates down to 75 grams per day at first, which would get them used to reading food labels. Counting calories could come later. I told them to get used to that, then eliminate or cut down considerably on sugar, mainly sweets like candy and bakery products, then switch from regular soda to diet, etc. Incremental change is possible with partisans, whereas radical change is not always realistic or practical.

Random Search and Trial-and-Error - A truly random search would mean that there is no systematic order to which possible solutions can be explored. A trial and error search is best applied to well-defined problems with few possible solution paths.

A random search for partisans usually means grasping at straws, or drawing from the knowledge of jailhouse lawyers and other know-it-alls, which isn't a very logical option. However, a trial and error process is usually within their grasp. A lot of recovering addicts go back to school, but not many of them finish. Many of them are attracted to the *idea* of going to college, but doesn't it make more sense to take one class first to test the waters, rather than going to all the trouble of applying (which in itself is time-consuming), filling out all those tedious financial aide forms, enrolling full time, and then finding out that it was all a big mistake to begin with, that they wasn't cut out for it? However, I don't recommend trying this with drugs, which so many addicts do. "Well, I'll just smoke pot and drink, and leave the meth alone. This trial and error process backfires repeatedly with DUIs, criminal charges, and a continued dependency on mind altering substances. In this area, partisans need, absolutely have to have, radical change.

Rules - Some problems, like *series* problems, depend on rules. Once the underlying principles are established, the problem is solved.

My example is very simple. If I am continually going to jail (a *series* of events) for violating the law, then I need to stop violating the law. Of course, if the problem is drug or alcohol oriented, then the problem is compounded, and the first rule would be to stop drinking or using. On the surface, this example seems superficial or obvious, but many of those who don't have any understanding whatever of the jointster population, thinks it's as easy as simply stop breaking the law or stop drinking or using. One of my friends' parents looked at me in earnest, and asked, "why doesn't Charlie just stop drinking?" I said, "because he can't." He replied with, "well you did it, why can't he?" Most people don't understand the dynamics of addiction, and the fact that most addicts are unable to accomplish it on a permanent basis. Remember, the available recovery options don't work very well, but that's all there is. Charlie wanted to be sober, but when he put sobriety on one end of the scale and drinking on the other, the drinking side weighed the most.

Brainstorming - This one can be fun. It's a method for group problem solving. I used this one when I facilitated groups at the rehab where I worked. It's not only fun, but it's effective. For example, in my group on change, I would ask the clients to brainstorm on the subject of triggers. Triggers, simply defined, are events that precipitate other events. All recovering addicts know what they are. If an alcoholic walks by a bar, he is inevitably going to be struck by the odors, which could serve as a trigger for relapse. An intravenous drug addict watching someone fix in a movie could also trigger a relapse. Anger is a very common trigger, which is why it is suggested that addicts not get too hungry, angry, lonely, or tired (HALT--another acronym). This reminds me of another acronym--FINE, which is often used when someone asks, how are you doing? The next time someone answers you with "fine," you might wonder if they're feeling **F**ucked up, **I**nsecure, **N**eurotic, and **E**motional. This acronym is usually used factitiously.

Restating the Problem - This is a useful strategy for ill-defined problems. In well-defined problems, the goal is usually explicitly stated in straightforward terms that leave little room for restatement.

Partisans, or anyone else for that matter, will often want to know how they can save money? They shop in discount markets, take coupons out of the newspapers, cut back on gas, and spend their weekends at home rather than going out. Suppose the problem is restated so it becomes, "How can I have more money?" Their solutions then change to such things as, getting a higher paying job, or moving to where rent is cheaper. Asking questions in different ways offers more options.

Analogies and Metaphors - Mythology and fairy tales have been assisting the human condition for hundreds of years. We can draw on alchemy for this one.

The prima materia in the alchemical vessel has to be destroyed before the transformation process can start taking place. Think of the old jointster self (in the dregs of addiction) as the prima materia that has to be destroyed, and the new recovered self as the finished product, the philosophers stone, individuation of the recovery process, the Gold.

Creativity: The notions of *unusual* or *unique*, and *good* or *useful*, are what's involved in creativity. It always involves judgement, and people may not agree on which actions or outcomes deserve to be labeled creative.

Not all creative people are alike either, which makes defining creativity a challenge and assessing it a monumental undertaking. The traditional psychological definition of creativity includes two parts: originality and functionality. You can't be creative unless you come up with something that hasn't been done before. The idea has to work, or be adaptive or be functional in some way. It has to meet some criteria of usefulness. There is a distinction to be made between creativity (lowercase c) and Creativity (uppercase C): creativity, which is often used as an indicator of mental health, which includes everyday cognitive functions (what I've been advocating here). Creativity, on the other hand, is far more rare. It occurs when a person solves a problem or creates an object that has a major impact on how other people think, feel, and live their lives. Mere creativity implies basic functionality. Creativity is something that people get Pulitzer and Nobel Prizes for.

≈ XII ≈

PERSONAL DEVELOPMENT

One of the complaints partisans will have is that they don't have time enough to do everything required of them. This is why time management strategies are essential.

<u>Time Management:</u> Time management skills are the abilities to recognize and solve personal time management problems. The goal of these techniques is to show what can be done to improve those skills.

With good time management skills partisans are in control of their time and their lives, of their stress and energy levels. They make progress at the workplace. They're able to maintain balance between work, personal, social, and family lives. They have enough flexibility to respond to surprises or new opportunities.

Developing time management skills are doable. Partisans will likely see improvement from simply becoming aware of the essence and causes of common personal time management problems. It's like addiction: once partisans recognize they have a problem, they can work on it. Without recognizing that there's a problem, then what is there to work on? With a time management program, partisans can better manage the areas that are most relevant for their situation. By just getting started, many of their problems gradually disappear. Partisans need to take this initiative on their own.

If partisans already know how they should be managing their time, but they still don't do it, then they have a case of mumpsimus (covered in chapter five). What partisans may be overlooking is the psychological side of their time management skills, psychological obstacles hidden behind their personalities.

Depending on personal situations, such obstacles may be the primary reason why they procrastinate, have difficulties saying no, delegating, or making time management decisions. The psychological component of their time management skills should also be dealt with.

<u>Time Management Tips:</u> Changing old habits into time management habits takes time and effort, and it's always easier when partisans have a simple system of practical rules and hints that are easy to keep in mind. The proven way to know what they want from their time is to set goals.

<u>Learn to know the difference between urgent and important</u>. The important tasks are those that lead partisans to their goals, and give them most of the long term progress and rewards. Those tasks are very often not urgent. Many urgent tasks are not really important, so partisans need to learn to know and respect their priorities. Aim to do the important things first. Remember the 80-20 rule: Eighty percent of reward comes from 20 percent of effort. One of the aims of these time management tips is to help partisans refocus their minds to give more attention and time to the most important 20 percent.

<u>Plan the actions for achieving goals</u>. Partisans should convert their goals into a system of specific actions to be done. The first significant point of planning is the planning process itself. It is a known fact, and partisans will see it for themselves, that the planning process stimulates their brains to come up with new efficient solutions, such as planning trips for errands. It programs their unconscious mind to search for shortcuts. It makes them much more prepared for each specific action. Besides, planning will help to identify potential conflicts and crises, minimizing the number of urgent tasks. Planning can also significantly lower the time spent on routine maintenance tasks, leaving more time for what they like to do or for what they think is important for their long term success.

Concentration for partisans can be easily lost in the sea of many boring or less important things waiting to be done. Students often find other things to do instead of homework. Undone things circulating in their mind are also a big drain of their mental energy.

When I was a student, I'd often find myself doing things that didn't really need to be done right away. This continued until one day I said out loud, "Wait a minute. I know what I'm doing. I'm putting off this paper." From then on I'd catch myself most of the time when that happened. It's amazing how we can manipulate ourselves.

I recommend that partisans keep a log for a specific time interval, like a week, and then analyze it to see where their time goes. For example, how much time is spent on *urgent* and *important* activities, and what people do they devote most of their time to? How much time do they spend thinking about drugs or alcohol? If those thoughts are still intruding, they need to be shoo'd away.

Time Management Exercise #1 - Becoming a better estimator:
Choose three tasks to work on this week. Write down an estimate of how long each task will take to complete. While working on these tasks, track the real time spent on each of them. At the end of the week, compare the estimates to

actual time spent. If they are within 20% of the estimate, then success has been achieved. If the estimate is beyond or below the 20% mark, look for reasons why there's an over or underestimate. Use insights to adjust estimates on the following week's projects. Repeat weekly for one month to improve the ability to estimate required task times.

Time Management Exercise #2 - An Exercise In Focus:
Take 15 minutes at the beginning of the next week and write down top priorities for the following seven days. List several items for each of life's most common arenas: work, family, community, and personal life. Post this list in a prominent spot where it can be seen every day. Pause for a moment to read the full list each morning. At the end of the week, review the list and calculate the number of tasks completed or moved forward. Attempt to maintain or improve that number each week.

Time Management Exercise #3 - Prime Time Log:
Identify prime time - that period of the day when it's the easiest to be productive and focused. Some people are early or mid morning people. Others are more alert in the afternoon or evening. Pick a two-hour slot during prime time. For one full week, keep a log of the tasks that was worked on during this time slot. Every 15 minutes during that prime time period, jot down the activity in the last quarter hour. At the end of the week, analyze the log. Calculate how much prime time was actually devoted to high priority tasks. Attempt to improve on that proportion the following week.

Eliminating procrastination:
Partisans should ask themselves the following questions:
- Have I ever seen my most important tasks being put off until later, and then later, and still later, while I'm getting busy with many, *not so important*, activities?
- Do I hope that I'll have more time and a better mood in the future to start something and do it properly?
- Does an approaching deadline mean a crisis for me?
- Do I keep hesitating every time I make a decision?

If partisans often see themselves in such low productivity situations, then there is a big chance that their lives have gotten under the control of the *procrastination* habit. A basic definition of procrastination is putting off the things that you should be doing now. This happens with most people to some degree. Yet, what makes a big difference for a partisan's successful recovery is the ability to recognize their procrastination reasons and expressions in their different forms, and to promptly get them under control, before this bad habit steals their opportunities, damages their career or self-worth, or destroys their relationships.

Causes of procrastination:
Here are some typical reasons why partisans procrastinate?
* Waiting for the right mood
* Waiting for the right time
* Lack of clear goals
* Underestimating the difficulty of the tasks
* Underestimating the time required to complete the tasks
* Unclear standards for the task outcomes
* Feeling as the tasks are imposed on you from outside
* Tasks are too ambiguous
* Underdeveloped decision making skills
* Fear of failure or fear of success
* Perfectionism

Goal Setting: When partisans know precisely what they want to achieve, they know where they have to concentrate their efforts. They'll also quickly spot the distractions that would otherwise lure them from their course, like the difference between what's urgent and what's important. By setting short-term goals and long-term goals, they are given a long-term vision with short-term motivation.

To give a broad, balanced coverage of all of the important areas in a partisan's life, they should try to set goals in some of these categories (or in categories of their own).

*Artistic: Do they want to achieve any artistic goals? If so, what?

*Attitude: Is any part of their mind-set holding them back? Do they sometimes behave in ways that make them feel uncomfortable with themselves? If so, set a goal to improve their behavior or find a solution to the problem.

* Career: What do they want to do as a career, and what level do they want to reach in their career?

* Education: Do they want to go to school? Or is there any knowledge they want to acquire in particular.

* Family: Do they want to become a parent? Do they want to become a better parent? How do they want to be seen by a partner or by members of their extended family?

* Financial: How ambitious are they? If they are ambitious, then how much do they want to earn in two years, five years, or ten years.

* Physical: Are there any athletic goals they want to achieve; for example, some type of athletic activity that they gave up. Or, do they just want to stay fit enough to be in good health in old age? What steps are they taking to achieve this?

* Pleasure: With drugs or alcohol no longer in their lives, how do they plan to enjoy themselves? It's essential that they ensure that some part of their life is *just for them*--not for their spouse or even their kids. It is pertinent that they make time for themselves.

* <u>Service to Others</u>: How are they going to be of service to others?

Here's a suggestion: Once partisans have set lifetime goals, they should set a 25-year plan of smaller goals. Then set a ten-year plan, a five-year plan, one year plan, six month plan, and a one month plan of progressively smaller goals that they should reach to achieve their ultimate lifetime goals. Each of these should be based on the previous plan. For any goals under a month, make a to-do list.

Decision Making: People are different, and so are their styles of decision making. Each person is a result of all of the decisions made in their life. Recognizing this, here are some tips to enhance decision making abilities.

1)   Partisans should not make decisions that are not theirs to make. Example: What if Jim says, "Hey Mike, get Fred to take out the trash and stay here and help me with my homework." Whereas that might be a humanitarian thing to do, it isn't Jim's decision.

2)   When making decisions, partisans are simply choosing from alternatives. They're not making a choice between right and wrong.
Let's say, for example, the only doctor in a rural community is out of town. A man's wife will die unless he can get her medication. The man calls the only drug store in town asking if he could get the drug without a prescription. The druggist says, "No, this medication requires a prescription." The man begs for his wife's life, but the druggist is adamant. The man has a decision to make: either let his wife die, or go to the drug store after it closes and break in and steal the medication. There are undoubtedly more alternatives, but there are times when partisans might think that those are the only options.

3)   Avoid snap decisions. Move fast on the reversible ones but more slowly on the non-reversible ones.
Partisans should check themselves when making snap decisions. If it's a decision that can't be reversed, then say, "wait a minute, let me think about this." How many of us have made decisions using emotional logic? How often does the inflated ego get in the way?

4)   Choosing the right alternative at the wrong time is not any better than the wrong alternative at the right time, so make the decision while there's still time.
Example: The application asks: Have you been convicted of a felony within the last seven years? Trying to be honest, a partisan would probably say no, but what if there was a felony conviction eight years ago. Why tell them that? If honesty is essential, then wait and tell them when or if there's an interview.

5)   Make decisions on paper. Write notes and keep ideas visible to consider all the relevant information in making the decision.

Obviously, this doesn't apply if it's a snap decision.

6)   Be sure to choose based on what is right, not who is right.
Liking one person better than another, doesn't make them right.

7)   Write down the pros and cons of a line of action. It clarifies thinking and makes for a better decision, much like journaling does.
Some partisans might not want to take the time to do this, but it's best to at least do it once to try it out.

8)   Don't let decisions accumulate. A backlog of many little decisions could be harder to deal with than one big and complex decision.
Besides that, procrastinating can cause forgetfulness and getting overwhelmed.

9)   Consider how others are affected by decisions. Whenever feasible, get them involved to increase their commitment.
A good example is spouses. Should anyone be making family decisions without consulting the family?

10) Recognize that it's not possible to know with 100% certainty that a decision is correct because the actions for carrying it out are to take place in the future.
In other words, make the decision and don't worry about it.

11) Remember that *not* making a decision is a decision.
It has been said that a decision should always be made at the lowest possible level and as close to the scene of action as possible. However, a decision should always be made at a level insuring that all activities and objectives affected are fully considered. The first rule tells us how far down a decision *should* be made. The second how far down it *can* be made.

12) Partisans should trust themselves to make decisions and then to be able to field the consequences appropriately.
In other words, be responsible for decisions by not placing the blame elsewhere. Remember, when a finger is pointing out, there's always at least three pointing back.

13) Don't waste time making decisions that don't have to be made.
This one especially applies to partisans. Why? Because, at some level, a vast majority of addicts are control freaks. They can't control their own lives, but they're experts at telling others how to control theirs.

14) Determine alternative courses of action before gathering data.
Work smarter not harder.

15) Before setting up what appears to be the best choice, assess the risk by asking "What can I think of that might go wrong with this alternative?"
Play the tape through . . .

16) Many decisions made are unimportant--about 80% of them. Establish operating limits and let subordinates or others make them.
That whole sentence can be said with one word: Delegate.

17) As part of the decision making process, always consider how the decision is to be carried out.
If I ask someone to clean the work area, I should probably be a little more specific. If most partisans are anything like me, they're going to do as little as they can get away with.

18) As soon as it's known that a decision will have to be made on a specific situation, review the facts at hand and then set it aside. Let this incubate for a while until it is time to finally make the decision.
In heuristic research, there's a process that starts with the *Initial Engagement* of the project, where everything is being put into perspective; The next part of the process is *Immersion*, where one is immersed in the project; After that is a period of what's called *Incubation*--a process in which the researcher retreats from the intense, concentrated focus on the project; Then, the researcher continues to the *Illumination, Explication*, and the *Creative Synthesis*. *Incubation* is the same thing this suggestion is making. Sometimes a partisan will need to back off from whatever they're doing and come back to it later. For example, the house key that has been misplaced often evades one's recall of its location while preoccupied with finding it. Almost as soon as one is absorbed in something else: "Oh yeah, I remember!"

19) Once the decision has been made, partisans need not look back. They should notice how it is currently affecting them and focus on their next move. Don't regret a decision. The best decision was made at the time. Focus on what is right now.
Basically, this is saying don't dwell on mistakes—get over it and go on.

20) Brainstorming with others often helps.
This always helps in making decisions, but partisans won't always have the time or access to people.

21) Discontinue prolonged deliberation about your decision. Make it and carry it through.
Don't beat on a dead horse—he's already dead. Once the decision is made, put the "what ifs" aside and go on.

Self Confidence: <u>Ensure that all the facts are known in advance</u>. It's best to do some research, and have it ready to produce (even give out copies if applicable). Bullies usually fail to prepare their facts; they dominate through bluster, force and reputation. If partisans know and can produce facts to support or defend a position, it is unlikely that the aggressor will have anything prepared in response. When it is known that a situation is going to arise, over which it would be good to have some influence, do research, calculate, get the facts and figures, solicit opinions and views, be able to quote sources; then one will be able to make a firm case, and also dramatically improve a reputation for being someone who is organized and firm.

Anticipate other people's behavior and prepare responses. Partisans can do imaginal dialogues for how things are likely to happen. They can prepare responses according to the different scenarios that they think could unfold. They can prepare other people for support and defense. Being well prepared will increase self-confidence and enable partisans to be assertive about what's important to them.

Prepare and use good questions to expose flaws in other people's arguments. Asking good questions is the most reliable way of gaining the initiative, and taking the wind out of someone's sails, in most situations. Questions that bullies dislike most are deep, constructive, incisive and probing, especially if the question exposes a lack of thought, preparation, consideration, consultation on their part. For example:
- What is your evidence (for what you have said or claimed)?
- Whom have you consulted about this?
- How did you go about looking for alternative solutions?
- How have you measured (whatever you say is a problem)?'
- How will you measure the true effectiveness of your solution if you implement it?
- What can you say about different solutions that have worked in other situations?

And don't be blown off. Stick to it. If the question is avoided or ignored, return to it, or re-phrase it (which can be prepared as well).

Partisans can re-condition reactions to dominant people, particularly by building 'triggered reactions,' giving themselves thinking time to prevent themselves from being bulldozed, and making like a brick wall in the face of someone else's attempt to dominate without justification. They can try visualizing themselves behaving in a firmer manner, saying firmer things, asking clear, probing questions, and presenting well-prepared facts and evidence. They can practice in their minds saying, "Hold on a minute, I need to consider what you've just said." They can also practice saying "I'm not sure about that. It's too important to make a snap decision now." Also "I can't agree to that at such short notice. Tell me when you really need to know, and I'll get back to you." There are other ways to help resist bulldozing and bullying.

Partisans can practice and condition new reactions in themselves to resist, rather than cave in, for fear that someone might shout or have a tantrum. If partisans are worried about their responses to being shouted at, then they can practice being shouted at until they realize it really doesn't hurt. It just makes the person doing the shouting look bad (mad, crazy, foolish, or stupid). Partisans can practice with their most scary friend shouting right in their face to "do as they're told," time after time, and in between each time say calmly (and believe it because it's true) "You don't scare me." Partisans can practice this until they can control their response to being shouted at.

Non assertive people have different styles and methods compared to dominant, aggressive people and bullies. Non assertive people are often extremely strong in areas of process, detail, dependability, reliability, finishing things (that others have started), checking, monitoring, communicating, interpreting and understanding, and working cooperatively with others. These capabilities all have the potential to undo a bully who has no proper justification. Partisans should find out what their strengths and styles are and use them to defend and support their positions. The biggest tantrum is no match for a well-organized defense.

Re-discover the belief that non assertive behavior is actually okay. It's the bullies who are the ones with the problems. Partisans who feel sympathy for someone who's threatening will psychologically put them in the ascendancy. Aggressors were often children who were not loved, or who were forced to live out the aspirations of their parents. It's suggested to be kind to them, because in many ways they are still children. Of course, partisans will have a hard time with this one.

Five Steps in Confidence Building

1. Concentrate on strengths rather than weaknesses. Confidence comes from within. Partisans have to concentrate on the positive things about themselves. Remember that the past is over; one can only change the future. Partisans should write down ten positive things about themselves.

Concentrate on potentials. These are the reasons partisans should love themselves and have high self-confidence. They need to give themselves credit for every positive thing they have written about themselves.

2. Make reminders of past successes. Confidence builds on past success. Because partisan had success before, they can (and will) have it again. We strengthen our confidence in any interest when we remind or review ourselves of past successes.

If partisans are trying to develop confidence in a new aspect, past success can still be useful in strengthening their confidence. For instance, if they had success in doing something new in the past, recall those experiences when trying something new, even if it is in a completely different part of their lives.

3. Take risks. Partisans should try doing things that they've never tried before.

It's always a bit of a challenge in doing new things, and just the act of accepting these challenges, some little and some big, whether they are successful or not, frequently improves self-confidence.

Partisans can approach new experiences as opportunities to learn, instead of occasions to win or lose. Doing so brings them new opportunities and can improve their sense of self-acceptance. Not doing so turns every possibility into an opportunity for failure, and inhibits personal development.

4. Use imaginal dialogues. Use this as an opportunity to contradict destructive beliefs. Then, partisans can remind themselves to "stop" and replace more realistic assumptions. For example, if they catch themselves expecting perfection, they can tell themselves through imaginal dialogues that they can't do everything perfectly, that it's only possible to try to do things and to try to do them well. This also allows them to accept themselves while still working to improve.

5. Visualize future success. Corporate executives, Olympic athletes, and successful people in all types of undertakings see future success. Confidence will increase when partisans visualize themselves succeeding. Think about it. If they know they will succeed, their confidence will rise.

Seeing future success does that very thing for us. Our minds cannot distinguish the difference between something real and something vividly imagined. So partisans should vividly visualize their success. What will it look like, smell like, taste like, and feel like to have succeeded? Who will be with them, what will they be hearing and where will they be? How will they be feeling at that instant? Placing this much vivid detail into their imagination increases the likelihood of success, and supports greater confidence!

≈ XIII ≈

RELAPSE PREVENTION

Everything in the previous chapter can be thought of as relapse prevention, and the same can be said about the chapter on thought discipline, but I think a concluding chapter on the more direct aspects of it would be helpful, especially for those in early recovery.

Relapse starts before one takes a drink or a drug, which is one of the critical reasons for so much education and work. Relapse is often triggered by the pain and discomfort of being clean and sober. There are symptoms of addiction that emerge when addicts first get clean. Unless addicts learn to manage these symptoms, they can increase in severity until they become as dysfunctional as they were when they were using. With alcoholics, they often become what's referred to as dry drunks. The same goes with drug addicts. They can be abstinent and still be as screwed up as they were when they was using. The symptoms can include an intensified awareness of sounds and sights, an overreaction to stress, emotional numbness, emotional overreaction, memory problems, dissociation, inability to focus, sleep disturbances, and/or mental confusion.

These symptoms can be controlled or minimized by learning as much about them as possible, by good nutritional practices and exercise, and by learning to relax and have fun. If the symptoms aren't managed, the stress can lead to a change in behavior, a breakdown in relationships and social ties, a loss of good judgment, and eventually out-of-control behavior. There are a lot of warning signs that lead to relapse. If partisans believe the relapse process begins with using drugs or alcohol and comes on without warning, they're less likely to recognize early warning signs. They're less likely to take care of themselves and learn to mange these symptoms before they become severe. If partisans aren't prepared for the warning signs, then relapse is a probable result.

Most addicts who relapse are not consciously aware of the warning signs while they're occurring. It's only when they look back later that they can recognize the things that were happening prior to picking up the first drink or drug. There are many reasons why addicts may be unaware of warning signs when they're happening.

A lack of information is a major warning sign. Addicts in early recovery don't know what to look for. Once partisans learn about relapse prevention, they can learn to recognize the symptoms and take action before they get out of control.

Another reason for relapse is neurological problems such as impairments of the brain and nervous system. These impairments create symptoms of mental confusion, emotional numbness or overreaction, memory problems, and stress sensitivity. In early recovery, these symptoms can create a fog that eventually improves in time.

Because those in early recovery are often unaware of the warning signs that lead back to active addiction, it's necessary that partisans talk regularly with friends or family who can help recognize warning signs. Also, just becoming aware of warning signs doesn't automatically enable partisans to interrupt them. They may not know what action to take to interrupt them. Warning signs develop slowly until they are overwhelming and become so severe that it affects their thinking, emotions, memory, judgment, and overall behavior. So even when warning signs are recognized, partisans might be unable to stop them even when they try.

For partisans who don't know what to do to interrupt warning signs, being educated in relapse prevention will help them learn. They can develop skills to interrupt the relapse process. Those who know what needs to be done but are unable to do it need people who will help them take the necessary steps. Some partisans might believe they *should* know what to do to interrupt warning signs. This can be an obstacle to asking for and receiving help. It also contributes to guilt when a loss of control occurs. Part of relapse prevention is using other people to stop warning signs when they start.

Here are a few myths concerning relapse:
* All that's needed is willpower and self-discipline to avoid relapse.
* Addicts who relapse are not motivated to recover.
* Chronic relapsers are hopeless because they're incapable of recovery.
* Just thinking about relapse will make it happen.
* It's impossible to interrupt relapse before hitting bottom again.

It is *not* a myth, however, that prescription drugs for legitimate uses are often precursors to relapse. The hypnotic class of drugs called barbiturates aren't prescribed any more for sleep disorders, but some anxiolytics are. The most common is the family of drugs known as the benzodiazepines. A recovering street-drug addict should know the dangers of flirting with addiction by accepting a doctor's prescription for a drug such as Xanax, regardless of what it's being prescribed for. Addiction to prescription drugs is still addiction; therefore, it's best to avoid controlled substances. However, there are times when severe pain is involved and only opiate pain killers will do the job. Prescription pain medication can be a major trigger, especially for recovering heroin addicts.

I had a friend who was in recovery back in the early nineties. Terry's drug of choice was heroin, but he'd been using meth for quite awhile because there was so much of it around and he usually didn't have to pay for it. As a result of his meth use, his teeth were in such bad shape, they all had to be extracted. Then he was fitted for dentures. He was prescribed some strong opiate pain relievers. Eventually the dentist wouldn't prescribe any more, and because of it, he went back to heroin or any other opiate that he could get his hands on. He can't afford a heroin or meth habit anymore, but he's still getting prescriptions for other controlled substances and buying them on the black market as much as his finances will allow. Would Terry have returned to active drug use had he not had dental problems? Knowing him as well as I do, I believe it was inevitable that he'd start using again, but many recovering addicts, who aren't as hard core as he, find it possible to take pain medication the way it's prescribed without returning to active addiction. When it comes to controlled substances, it's best to tread softly, and then discontinue their use as soon as possible.

I'd be remiss if I didn't reiterate the dangers of associating with old drinking and using buddies.

Friends: A couple months after I was cut loose from prison, my old friend, Jack, was also released, so I gave him a call. That evening I went to his mom's house for a visit. We made small talk for a few minutes and then he went to the restroom. After being in there for about five minutes, I knew what he was doing, so I tapped on the bathroom door. He said, "I'll be right out, Johnny."

I said, "Leave a little in the cotton for me."

"Are you sure?"

When I said yes, he opened the door, and then we both fixed. I knew I wasn't going to start anything that would result in a heroin habit, because heroin was never my drug of choice. Getting high with him, I rationalized, was a one-time thing and I didn't see any point in setting a new clean date, which is what we're supposed to do when we relapse. With Jack and me being the only ones who knew, my secret was safe.

I'd read and studied about relapse prevention in prison. I knew the danger signs, and I knew that associating with old friends, hanging on to paraphernalia, and going to old haunts was a threat to remaining clean and sober. I justified the fix by telling myself that it wasn't a relapse. My definition of a relapse was drinking or using on a continual basis. I told myself that I'd remain abstinent after that one time. What I hadn't internalized, although I heard the phrase numerous times, is that our addiction is cunning, baffling, and powerful. The next day I beat myself up pretty badly. *I'm supposed to be honest, even to myself. I don't even like heroin that much. What's wrong with me?* The guilt really starting eating at me.

During my dump scavenging days when I was on meth, I accumulated three big trash cans full of copper wire and needed someone to help me burn the insulation off and then take me somewhere to sell it. Jack knew how to go about all that, and he had a little pick-up truck to haul it in. A couple months after my supposedly one-time relapse, I offered him half the money if he'd help me burn and sell it. When he came to the house, he greeted my mom, and we made small talk in the living room for a few minutes. Then he excused himself to use the rest room. When he didn't come out right away, I walked over and tapped lightly on the door.

Yeah, "he said in a low voice so not to alarm my mom."

In a likewise voice I replied, "Save me a cotton." Then I returned to the living room, sat down and started chatting with my mom again.

A minute or two later, I heard the door open and Jack said out loud, "Hey Johnny, c'mere for a minute."

I went in and he handed me a loaded syringe. I fixed, returned to the living room, and sat down. Because I was able to do it in less than 10 seconds, my mom was none the wiser. At least that's what I thought.

Again I started beating myself up: *Why am I doing this? My fucking life will go down the shitter again if I keep this shit up. I have to come to terms with this. What am I gonna do? This makes the second time. Well . . . there's only one thing to do: if I do it one more time, since a third time establishes a pattern, I will set a new clean date.*

When Herby came to Barstow for a visit from Australia a few months later, I still hadn't internalized that crucial precept of not going around old friends, because me, Herby, and another friend spent the entire weekend slamming meth. That was the third time, so I honored the pact I made with myself. I thought I'd learned that lesson, and since I learned it the hard way, I was convinced I'd never be tempted again. So, the most meaningful thing I can say about this, is that it hasn't been necessary for me to take a drink or put a needle in my arm since 7 May 1990, and for that I am everlastingly grateful. However....

I'd been clean and sober for more than two years when I went to my 30-year class reunion in 92. Since I'd been clean for so long, I didn't think I'd be affected by being around old high school buddies who I drank with so long ago. I didn't relapse, but I really wanted to. After that, I was thoroughly convinced that I could no longer go around my old friends and haunts or hang on to paraphernalia.

Paraphanelia: Some partisans in early recovery will be reluctant to let go of bongs, pipes, and other drug paraphernalia, as well as T-shirts, posters, and bumper stickers that brandish brand-name beer, wine, and liquor. Back in the 60s, before disposable syringes came out, we used binkies to fix with. In those days, just the needles were sold in pharmacies for diabetics. We'd buy a bottle of Murine Eye Drops, throw the bottle away, and keep the plastic eyedropper. A needle would fit perfectly on the end of it. By putting the needle in a wet cotton with the eyedropper's plunger squeezed, the eyedropper would fill up when we let go of the plunger. I kept a binkie for a long time as a novelty.

There's no getting around the fact that hookers are slippery associations. They're not directly drug-related associations, but where there's hookers, drugs aren't very far away and usually accessible to hookers, and addicts know that.

What about music, books, movies, and television? To this day when I hear certain songs, I am automatically taken back to my bartending days. I had some really good times where I worked and those songs were reminders that could've been triggers in early recovery if my head wasn't in the right place. There's not much one can do about what's being played in public, but partisans would be wise to consider not getting trigger music, books, and movies. Why take the chance?

Haunts: It's not uncommon for those in early recovery to justify going into bars to shoot pool, throw darts, play shuffleboard, or other types of games. They convince themselves that they can handle it because drinking and using isn't what they're going there for. There's a cliche around 12-step programs: If you repeatedly go into a barber shop, eventually you'll get a haircut. I think the analogy is rather silly, but it gets the point across, because a relapse is inevitable if partisans patronize establishments where alcohol is sold. For the most part, those are also places where drug trafficking occurs.

Continually thinking about drugs and alcohol, and everything associated is one thing, but it's common for many in early recovery to be talking about it with others. If partisans talk about it a lot, how is it possible to stop thinking about it? It's not. Hopefully, by the time partisans complete the ten stages of recovery, they will have successfully eliminated drug and alcohol related thought patterns.

When I was facilitating groups in the rehab I worked at, I explained the process I went through when I was shooing away thoughts while I was in prison. Several clients were impressed, but I'd have to remind those very clients that they were still continually having drug-related conversations, because I'd catch them at it. I reminded a few of them several times, but I came to realize that it wasn't doing any good. Most of those clients were forced to be there, either by a judge, drug court, probation, or family. Partisans have to be totally committed to recovery before such an undertaking can be successful.

How do partisans say no? By discussing potential problems regarding drug refusal and exploring methods for handling various situations.

Work Situations: Invitations from co-workers to go to the bar after work isn't uncommon, and the frequency usually depends on the type of employment it is. There's a lot of drinking going on after work in the construction trades. White collar employment, which pertains to the ranks of office and professional workers typically have business trips, meetings, seminars, and other gatherings that involve drinking and sometimes drug use. More typical are scenarios where entertaining clients is involved.

If partisans are married and it's an after-work scenario, then it's easy enough to opt out because of familial obligations. But it's another matter if partisans are expected to entertain clients or potential clients who could be financially advantageous to the company the partisan works for. Regardless of the circumstances of employment, excuses will only last so long, which is why partisans need to come out and say something like, "No thanks, bro. For me one is too many and a thousand isn't enough." Statements to that effect get the point across.

If co-workers refuse to accept a partisan's obligation to recovery, then they're not worth arguing with. Simply saying no to them is enough, and if they insist, then the time is right to get rude by saying something like, "Look, I said I don't want a drink (or drug). What part of No don't you understand." Most people, however, in the professional work force respect those in recovery and will usually stand by and encourage them.

Social Situations: There are as many reasons for having parties as there are reasons to drink and use, but holiday parties such as Christmas and new year's eve, birthday parties, and retirement parties are more common. Partisans in early recovery are going to be hard pressed to not drink or use drugs at parties where they're expected to show up. Family members expect family members to be there. Employers expect employees to be there. Close friends expect their friends to be there. If partisans are unable to get out of attending a party, and someone offers them a drink that knows they're in recovery, they can try humorous responses like, "No thanks, but can I offer you a glass of arsenic?" or "Why bother? I can get the same effect just by taking off my glasses or holding my breath for ten seconds."

The traditional college education is rife with parties and other drinking and using scenarios. Getting accepted to a major university is an honor and therefore much more difficult for partisans to excuse themselves from campus activities where drugs and alcohol are ubiquitous. Most partisans who plan on going back to school have other options that the major university students don't have. Non-traditional education, especially online programs are becoming much more preferable for many reasons.

The ten stages of development is a way to recover from addiction to drugs and alcohol, but chapter twelve on should be used as a reference guide. There's a lot of useful information there that partisans would be wise to refer to periodically. This approach won't be for everybody, but it's an option for those who take issue with all the God talk in 12-step programs. It's also an option for those who live in rural areas who don't have access to other recovery options like counseling, etc. For those interested in reading my other books, they are: (i) *Scumbag Sewer Rats: An Archetypal Understanding of Criminalized Drug Addicts.* (ii) *Addict to Academic: Recovery From 30 Years of Drug Addiction.* (iii) *Addiction Papers: From the Perspective of Depth Psychology.* All of these books are available online at Amazon and Barnes & Nobel, or they can be ordered at any bookseller. For those interested in contacting me, here is my contact info:

John E. Smethers, Ph.D.
Phone: 760-256-8266
Email: ScumbagSewerRats@verizon.net
Website: www.JohnSmethers.com

References

Alcoholics Anonymous World Services, Inc. *Alcoholics anonymous: The story of how many thousands of men and women have recovered from alcoholism*. 4th ed. (2001). New York: Alcoholics Anonymous World Services, Inc.

Alice. (January, 1996). *How many recover from alcohol and drug abuse annually*. In Go Ask Alice. Retrieved January 5, 2008 from http://www.goaskalice.columbia.edu/0763.html).

Eliade, M. (1958). *Rites and symbols of initiation: The mysteries of birth and rebirth*. New York: Harper& Row Publishers.

Gilchrist, C. (1998). *The elements of alchemy*. Rockport, MA: Element Books Limited.

James, W. (1958). *The varieties of religious experience*. New York: The Penguin Group.

Raff, J. (2000). *Jung and the alchemical imagination*. York Beach, Maine: Nocolas-Hays, Inc.

Ross, R. (April, 1986). *Three nation umbrella org. to aid Jewish prison inmates, families*. In National Jewish Press. Retrieved December 30, 2001 from www.rickross.com/reference/Jewpris5.html (now defunct).

von Franz, M. L. (1980). *Alchemy: An introduction to the symbolism and the psychology*. Toronto, Canada: Inner City Books.

www.ingramcontent.com/pod-product-compliance
Lightning Source LLC
Chambersburg PA
CBHW060909280326
41934CB00007B/1244